Beyond
the
angry
black

By John A. Williams:

Beyond the angry black (edited)

This is my country too

Sissie

Africa, her history, lands and people

The angry black (edited)

Night song

The angry ones

Beyond the angry black

Edited by
John A. Williams

Cooper Square Publishers
New York
1966

Dedication

For Herbert A. "Hoppy" Johnson, Syracuse, New York, who let the jail doors close without many of us behind them; and for his time and patience; his kindness and wisdom; for all these things which our fathers wouldn't or couldn't give to us.

Thanks.

Contents

Introduction to the second edition   *xi*

Introduction to the first edition   *xvii*

James Baldwin	*Theatre: The negro in and out of it*	*2*
Gwendoyn Brooks	*Medger Evers*	*11*
Juniuȿ Edwards	*Mother dear and daddy*	*13*
Hoyt W. Fuller	*The apostle*	*24*
John Howard Griffin	*Dark journey*	*41*
Chester Himes	*Dilemma of the negro novelist in the United States*	*51*
Langston Hughes	*Name in print*	*59*
Shirley Jackson	*Flower garden*	*62*
Abram Kardiner and Lionel Ovesey	*Psychodynamic inventory of the negro personality*	*86*
Seymour Krim	*Ask for a white cadillac*	*102*
S. P. Lomax	*Pollution*	*118*
Dennis Lynds	*A night in Syracuse*	*125*
John W. McReynolds	*Memo to the current madness*	*138*
G. C. Oden	*Man white, brown girl and all that jazz*	*143*
Paul Olsen	*Line of duty*	*145*
Margaret Walker	*Now*	*155*
John A. Williams	*Navy black*	*157*
Richard Wright	*The plea*	*173*
Carrie Allen Young	*Adjö means goodbye*	*191*

A postscript concerning the times   *197*

Acknowledgements

James Baldwin | Theatre: The Negro In and Out of It
Copyright 1961, by Urbanite Publishing Company. Reprinted by permission of The Urbanite.

Gwendolyn Brooks | Medgar Evers
Copyright Chicago Magazine 1964, New Chicago Foundation. Reprinted by permission of Chicago Magazine.

Junius Edwards | Mother Dear and Daddy
Mother Dear and Daddy. Copyright 1962, 1966, John A. Williams.

Hoyt W. Fuller | The Apostle
Copyright, 1966, John A. Williams.

John Howard Griffin | Dark Journey
from *Black Like Me* by John Howard Griffin. Copyright, 1960, 1961, John Howard Griffin. Reprinted by permission of Houghton Mifflin Co.

Chester Himes | Dilemma of the Negro Novelist in the United States
Dilemma of the Negro Novelist in the United States. Copyright, 1966, John A. Williams.

Langston Hughes | Name in Print
from *Simple Stakes a Claim*. Reprinted by permission of Harold Ober Associates, Inc.

Shirley Jackson | Flower Garden
from *The Lottery*. Copyright 1949, Shirley Jackson. Reprinted by permission of Farrar, Straus and Giroux, Inc.

Abram Kardiner, Lionel Ovesey | Psychodynamic Inventory of the Negro Personality
Copyright 1951, W. W. Norton & Co., Inc. 1955, Abram Kardiner. Reprinted by permission of the author.

Introduction
to the second edition

THIS COLLECTION was first published in 1962 with 12 contributors. Now there are 19. That seven of these are white authors is significant, I think, for what ties this collection together, what makes for its theme, quite simply is the Negro in America. Since it is historical fact that white America began spinning the cobwebby dilemma in which we live today, it is fitting that white American writers are actively concerned with undoing the past by calling attention to the wrongs in the present.

But with such a theme can this anthology be considered literature?

As I understand literature, it must be universal. Suffering is universal; oppression by one group over another is universal and today there is not a single nation in the world that does not know that our failure to solve our racial dilemma is our long-standing and major weakness.

Literature must have permanence. Our problem has been with us for half a thousand years—since the 15th century, since only a few years after the recognized discovery of America by Columbus.

Literature must have form and expression, therefore, the works of the contributors must speak for themselves through their fiction, articles and poems. It is the burning concensus of most of white America that writing by or about Negroes is all the same; that the voices are always in harmony, have but one pitch and sing but one song. Nothing could be more untrue. Each contributor has his song and though the chorus may be a mighty swelling thundering injustice, each has arrived at this point through personal experience or concern.

When this collection was first put together back in 1962, there had been no large scale civil rights demonstrations. People murdered while driving the highways of the South received no more attention than an inch of copy in most of the newspapers in the nation. The police dogs used to attack men, women and children were part of an out-of-focus image very much related to the German concentration camps of World War II. While we feared the annual approach of school openings in the Fall, particularly although not confined to the South, we had not yet come to fear the approach of summer and rioting. Nearly every work in the first edition of this collection indicated the smouldering presence of The Angry Black.

In my introduction to that first edition I spoke of reason and of the Civil War centennial celebration. And I spoke of truth. What whimsey! But, perhaps by the time we celebrate the bi-centennial of the Civil War we will have truth; we will have reason. If not, we will have nothing. In order to nail down truth we must admit that our problems are deep and ugly and gnarled. It almost seems that the laws initiated by men of goodwill and desired by men of goodwill have been set in motion too late. We have accepted laws passed without really considering why they were necessary in the first place.

Can black Americans really be expected to understand why the leaders of this nation pressed for fair trials for Nazi war criminals, many of whom were responsible for the deaths of millions, while at the same time those leaders failed so miserably and consistently to provide that same safeguard for black Americans who committed no crime at all?

That is an example of the bitter reasoning going on today. However much men try to reason, the old atavism of the Negro persists. The remembered legacy of hate and fear; of deprivation and humiliation of exploitation in every sphere, bar none, of human life has exploded into the battle cry:

"GET WHITEY!"

And nearly everyone pretends not to know why.

Then allow these writers to tell you why. This is a step toward reason.

"The figure of the Negro," writes JAMES BALDWIN, who since last appearing in these pages has published three books and had two plays produced on Broadway, "is at the very heart of the American confusion." Baldwin's article, *Theatre: The Negro In and Out of It* today finds the Negro more in than he was in 1962.

But each gain is made at great cost, as Pulitzer Prize poet, GWENDOLYN BROOKS tells us in *Medgar Evers,* a poem that merges life with death, an every day happening, but finds in that merging: "Roaring no rapt arise-ye to the dead he/Leaned across tomorrow. People said that/he was holding clean globes in his hands." The poem

also reminds us that, while Evers met death, his killer outan justice—
and the pursuit of reason must therefore continue.

Even as Negroes and whites charge the barriers of prejudice
Negroes themselves exercise an unholy degree of prejudice within the
race, as JUNIUS EDWARDS points out in *Mother Dear and Daddy*.
This is another part of white America's "legacy." The øctaroon looks
down on the quadroon; the quadroon sniffs at the mulatto; the mulatto looks down on the brown and the brown despises the black.

Standing just outside this cage Negroes make for themselves is the
white man. HOYT FULLER'S *The Apostle* marks this Madison Avenue
model who continually calls up the wrong image of the Negro. The
image of course, is his own. Money? Prestige? Free samples, anyone?
But the image isn't in focus for when *The Apostle* speaks, it is with
sense; without selfishness. It is *The Apostle* who in the end is driving
the bargain. This is a chilling story because, with the white man's
image of the Negro shattered there is the implied threat of retaliation
by the him against the Negro. But terror is much at the root of Negro
life in America anyway.

All are at the mercy of the terror of the South of which JOHN
HOWARD GRIFFIN writes. Since this volume was last issued, youths,
women, children, Army officers and a few others, have met this terror
face to face but have not been as lucky as Griffin. They never lived to
write a *Dark Journey*.

Some, knowing of this naked fear, and knowing of the paralyza-
tion of the American moral, have fled the nation in disgust. CHESTER
HIMES has lived in Paris for a good many years, after spending over
40 years in America. His article, *Dilemma of the Negro Novelist in the
United States* is Himes' first major article to appear in the U.S. in
almost 15 years.

LANGSTON HUGHES also goes away from home very often—
but he returns; Harlem is his home and all the evil seems incapable
of driving him away. Instead, he reminds us to smile from time to time
and, when we get to the point where we become "leaders" or "spokes-
men," he recalls for us that his character, Simple, is as constant as 7th
Avenue.

We are only now taking note of the great physical and mental
pressures exerted upon whites involved in seeking a solution to our
dilemma—a white Georgia attorney is run out of town for urging
compliance with the Civil Rights Act; a white civil rights worker is
beaten; another brutally murdered. Others are shot down in the bright

glare of a noonday sun. The late SHIRLEY JACKSON sets her story, *Flower Garden* in Vermont. Here too, among the gentle mountains and the velvet green, pressures exist. They are not as cruel as in Georgia, but they are just as effective. The *Flower Garden* is the symbol of beauty two kinds of people—Mrs. MacLane and her Negro gardener, Mr. Jones—can achieve working together. But the garden is destroyed by a great tree that falls on it during a storm. The great tree is symbolic of old and deep rooted hatred and superstition; the tree is the neighbors' and their gossip and "social" cruelty. The fate of Mrs. MacLane seems to be that of the person of goodwill, running from the task, tired of it, embittered with it for, at the end of the story, Mrs. MacLane speaks to Mr. Jones who pulls futilely at the fallen tree: "Leave it alone, Mr. Jones. Leave it for the next people to move!"

It is possible that, if the sociologists, the government specialist and statisticians had read *Mark Of Oppression* (and a host of other works) first published in 1951, no "tree" would be laying today in the flower garden. They did not. *Psychodynamic Inventory of the Negro Personality* is still the answer most people come up with. In it, one finds the cause for unrest, anger, if you will, the cry for the truth of the promise. And if one can find cause for anger, nearby must be the cause for peace. *Inventory* is the work of DRS. ABRAM KARDINER & LIONEL OVESEY.

Certainly there will not be peace if a romanticized image of the Negro, cloaked in intellectual sagacity persists. This is what SEYMOUR KRIM has done in *Ask For a White Cadillac*. Knowing Krim, I am aware that he was sincere; more than that, he *is* sincere. But his observations in the final analysis, make it hard to accept the real Negro—if there is such a creature.

S. P. LOMAX's *Pollution* was made into a short Dutch film and attracted widespread attention throughout Europe. Of the white Americans he can only say, "Everything they touch. Everything! (They pollute.)"

DENNIS LYNDS' *A Night in Syracuse* is a haunting, insinuating work. Lynds first wrote it some years ago and when this collection was going into a new edition we recalled it. This story is about pain, but not the kind a doctor can do anything about. And it is about a weary kind of love. There is no basic racial theme here. All the characters seem predictably, tired of race and its burdensome by-products. The most pathetic character in the story is the one who does employ racial epithets. And he is monumentally pitied.

JOHN W. McREYNOLDS will admit to no pity in *A Memo to the Current Madness*. In sear language he tells us what the white man has done to the Negro in America and when and how. But he tells the Negro that whatever his due he must take it—his natural dignity, his role in America—and the sooner the better so the white man can reclaim the soul he lost in the process of making the Negro a second-class American.

G. C. ODEN in *Man White, Brown Girl and All That Jazz* sets an interracial love affair to poetry. The beginning lines are memorable: "It is essential I remember/ ours was a fair exchange." At the poem's end without rancor, without resorting to the easy, bitter racial props, she concludes, "You found your clearing:/ I fathom mine./ We have had the best of it."

For all the burdens of racial hatreds, Negroes have always fought in America's wars. And in all the wars the Negro soldier has had two enemies—the one in front of him, the Japanese, the German, the British, the Chinese, the Viet Cong. Beside him and behind him is the other, the white American soldier, his comrade in arms. Set in Korea, PAUL OLSEN's *Line of Duty* sadly reminds us of the stories of World Wars I and II. We are jolted to find that racial antipathies between white and black American troops exist today in Viet Nam.

Now, MARGARET WALKER's poem, speaks eloquently for itself: "Time to wipe away the slime/ time to end this bloody crime." There is a strong relationship between this poem and McReynolds article; both cut through the obvious: the need for jobs and homes; both drive to the heart of the matter, human dignity. This is fitting for Miss Walker is Negro, McReynolds white and both are Southerners. Both call for the need to free people from the performances of undignified acts.

More and more the works of RICHARD WRIGHT have come to have urgent meaning today. Reading some of the current works, one thinks back to Wright and all he wrote over a quarter of a century ago and suddenly it seems that nothing new is being said at all because Wright said it all. In *The Plea* Mr. Max in his summation before the court echoes the growing belief that white America can never be free until the black American is loosed from bondage, economic and spiritual.

Adjö Means Goodbye is CARRIE ALLEN YOUNG's first published work. It is a story about children, but it is also a story that stingingly underlines the precise moment when children discover they are black children or white children. It is the moment they discover America.

A novel, now in progress, was born from my story, *Navy Black.*

John A. Williams
Barcelona, Spain
May, 1966

Introduction
to the first edition

WHAT LIES beyond anger I hope is reason. I do not mean to say that anger is a useless emotion; the adrenalin it manufactures has saved lives. Anger makes us terribly aware that something is wrong because it does not spring wantonly out of air; it has an originating cause. But anger also blinds and thereby limits and weakens; it cripples those who suffer it, and in the end, those who've caused it. Each selection in this collection is a probe beyond anger, a reaching for reason; a search for the reasons which have given rise to the anger —largely black anger—only just now viewed full face in these United States. There is other than black anger and it has come because other than black people also see that whatever future America will have will be directly related to the solving of its racial dilemma, which is, basically, a human dilemma.

The moral and imperative question: What view shall the Negro be seen in has been asked since before Melville. It is a question which we, approaching the 100th anniversary of the Emancipation Proclamation, have answered only by default; Civil War Centennial celebrations undoubtedly will continue until April, 1965. If anything, the celebrations have been marked by the striking absence of the role of the Negro in the Civil War; this is the answering by default which is still practiced. It is most imperative that the Negro be seen and seen as he is; the morality of the situation will then resolve itself, and truth, which is what we all presumably are after, will then be served. This done we may all be able to rid ourselves of the illusion and delusion with which we've lived for so long a time. Since we can now calculate the end of our time—today, say, or tomorrow—we are required to extend our time by doing away with the cancers which have shown us quite clearly where the end of time is. Do not think nor believe that the problem of black and white in America has no relationship to what has brought us very close to the American twilight. Over the centuries the sheer energy of creating a valley for the Negro to stay in has drained us of untold ideas; has cost us billions of dollars; has branded the American dream, LIE. The energy inherent in denying the Negro has pierced every facet of American life, has influenced thought both here and abroad.

The selections here tell of erosion and its effect upon white as well as black. Few of these pieces are neat or pretty subjects, but what is here is the mirror of our time and place and therefore the legitimate concern of writers who live in it.

As the Negro is, who is sure? He is hardly seen upon our image projectors. James Baldwin outlines not only the predicament of the Negro actor in theatre, but the affect of his absence upon white actors, entertainment and art and the whole of America. Mr. Baldwin's selection is *Theatre: The Negro In and Out of It*.

Negroes, having been deprived of values of their own as a race, have by necessity, come to have values which are identical to those of the whites. The basic accoutrement, therefore, is the fortune to have a light skin. Junius Edwards tells us in his *Mother Dear and Daddy* of the effects of white upon black, even to children.

One of the most potent side effects of prejudice meted out from white to black is the Negro's self-hatred of himself; he is despised; he despises himself. Sometimes, as in Ralph Ellison's *The Death of Clifton*, this cycle ends in self-destruction.*

Disguised as a Negro, John Howard Griffin gets to the root of the problem as he describes in *Dark Journey* an eerie, unbelievable journey along a Mississippi road, when all the illnesses of the South were unleashed upon him.

In a lighter vein Langston Hughes' quick, satiric pen observes for his famous Simple, the contrived absence of the Negro from daily life to which he is so much committed in *Name in Print*.

Shirley Jackson against the backdrop of New England paints a racial prejudice which seems as insidious as a snake: attractively colored, elusive, almost untouchable. Miss Jackson's horror is that of the helplessness of people no longer in communication with one another.

But it is through the excerpt from *Mark of Oppression*, a quiet American classic, *Psychodynamic Inventory of the Negro Personality*, that we are able to observe the effects of discrimination upon Negroes. This selection is from a case study of the Negro in Harlem. Dr. Kardiner reveals a Harlem which is a psychic concentration camp and not at all the glittering playground many whites feel it is even

---

* Not included in 2nd edition.

today. It is by alphabetical arrangement that Seymour Krim's *Ask For a White Cadillac* follows.

Another side effect of discrimination is the schism which has come between black men and black women. S. P. Lomax has created a small mental war between a Negro woman and a socially emasculated Negro man; the woman, in order to truly be one, has chosen a white mate. Mr. Lomax's story is called *Pollution*.

Americans take their vices with them wherever they go. In Korea, where Paul Olsen's story is set, we find even in that war-torn land a microcosm of the struggle of black and white, of uncertainty, of an aggressive passivity.

Richard Wright, the first Angry Man did not know the meaning of passiveness. His love for America was obscured by his hatred of it; but love there was or he would not have railed against her as he did. Mr. Wright's *The Plea*, anticipates by several years the ideas of psychiatrists involved in race relations.

These then, together with my own story, *Son in the Afternoon*,* are the selections for THE ANGRY BLACK.

John A. Williams
New York City, 1962

* Not included in 2nd edition.

Beyond
the
angry
black

James Baldwin

is the author of three novels, two collections of essays and most recently, a collection of short stories *Going to Meet the Man*. Two of his plays, *Blues for Mr. Charlie* and *The Amen Corner* were produced on Broadway; the latter has been seen throughout the world.

Theatre: the negro in and out of it

IT IS a sad fact that I have rarely seen a Negro actor really well used on the American stage or screen, or on television. I am not trying to start an artificial controversy when I say this, for in fact most American performers seem to find themselves trapped very soon in an "iron maiden" of mannerisms.

Somehow, the achieved record falls below the promise. Henry Fonda, for example, is one of the accomplished actors around, but I find it very difficult to watch him because most of the roles he plays do not seem to me to be worth doing.

Moreover, it would seem to me that his *impulse* as an actor is very truthful; but the roles he plays are not. His physical attributes, and his quality of painful, halting honesty are usually at the mercy of some mediocre playwright's effort to justify the bankruptcy of the American male, e.g., the nebbish with whom he so gallantly struggles in *Two For The Seesaw*.

The point is that one can attend the Broadway theatre, and most of the Off-Broadway theatre all season long without ever being moved, or terrified, or engaged.

The spectacle on the stage does not attempt to recreate our experience—thus helping us to deal with it. The attempt is almost always in the opposite direction: to justify our fantasies, thus locking us within them.

Now, the figure of the Negro is at the very heart of the American confusion. Much of the American confusion, if not most of it, is a direct result of the American effort to avoid dealing with the Negro as a man. The theatre cannot fail to reflect this confusion, with results which are unhealthy for the white actor, and disastrous for the Negro.

The character a white actor is called on to play is usually a wishful fantasy: the person, not as he is, but as he would like to see himself. It need scarcely be said, therefore, that the situations the playwright invents for this person have as their principal intention the support of this fantasy.

The Caine Mutiny Court Martial, A Majority of One, Tea and Sympathy, and *Tall Story,* are all utterly untruthful plays. The entire purpose of the prodigies of engineering skill expanded on them is to make the false seem true. And this cannot fail, finally, to have a terrible effect on the actor's art, for the depths out of which true inspiration springs are precisely the depths he is forbidden to reach.

I am convinced that this is one of the reasons for the nerve-wracking *busyness* of our stage—"Keep moving, maybe nobody will notice that nothing's happening,"—and the irritating, self indulgent mannerisms of so many of our actors. In search of a truth which is not in the script, they are reduced to what seem to be psychothera-peutic exercises.

Listening to actors talk about the means they employ to "justify" this line, or that action, is enough to break the heart and set the teeth on edge. Sometimes the actor finds that no amount of skill will "justify" or cover up the hollowness or falsity of what he is called on to do. This is where the director comes in: it would seem that much of his skill involves keeping everything moving at such a clip, and to have so many things happening at once, that the audience will remain, in effect, safely protected from the play.

If this is true for the white actor, it is unimaginably worse for the Negro actor. The characters played by white actors, however untruthful they may essentially be, do depend—indeed, *must* depend —on the accumulation of small, very carefully observed detail. Thus, Chester Morris, playing a thoroughly unreal father, in *Blue Denim*, yet mimics the type so well that it is easy to be misled into believing that you once knew someone like him. But the characters played by Negro actors do not have even this advantage. White people do not know enough about Negro life to know which details to look for, or how to interpret such details as may have been forced on their attention.

To take one of many possible examples: the scene in Reginald Rose's *Black Monday*, in which Juano Hernandez is beaten to death. Hernandez plays a janitor in the Deep South, you will remember, who is opposed to integration. He does not believe—so he informs a marvelously mocking and salty Hilda Sims—in pushing himself in "where he is not wanted." He is also telling this to his twelve year old grandson, who is now beginning (somewhat improbably) to wonder if he is as good as white people.

Now, of course, we have all met such janitors and such Negroes. But their tone is very different and their tone betrays what they really feel. However servile they may appear to be, there is always a murderous rage, or a murderous fear, or both, not quite sleeping at the very bottom of their hearts and minds. The truth is that they do not have any real respect for white people: they despise them and they fear them. They certainly do not trust them. And when such a man confronts his nephew or his grandson, no matter what he says, there cannot fail to be brought alive in him envy and terror and love and hate. He has always hated his condition, even though he feared to change it, even though he may no longer be able to admit it.

If the playwright does not know this, as on the evidence, I gather Mr. Rose did not, he cannot draw the character truthfully and the actor who plays him is seriously handicapped.

This shows very painfully in the scene in which Hernandez meets his death. His reaction to the effigy of a hanged Negro, in spite of all Mr. Hernandez's skill, is false. This is not the first time he has seen such an effigy, and if he has been living in that town all his life, it is simply not possible for the white people there to surprise him—at least, they cannot surprise him by being wicked or by being afraid. They have always been that, and he knows that about them, if he knows nothing else. Any Negro, facing, in such a town, three over-heated white boys, knows what he is in for.

He can try to outwit, flatter, cajole them, put them at their ease by humiliating himself—though at this point, the spectacle of his humiliation is probably not enough to set them at their ease; or if the chips are really, at last, thank heaven, down, he can resolve to take one of them with him. And even if all the foregoing guesswork is wrong, one thing remains indisputable: once attacked, he would certainly not be trying to get past his attackers in order to go to work. Not on that morning, not in that school, not with death staring at him out of the eyes of three young white men.

All of the training, therefore, all of the skill which Mr. Hernandez has acquired, to say nothing of his talent—for it took a vast amount of talent to bring Lucas, in *Intruder In The Dust* alive—is here not merely wasted, which would be bad enough; it is subverted, sabo-taged, put at the mercy of a lie; for the well-spring on which the actor must draw, which is his own sense of life, and his own experience, is precisely, here, what Mr. Hernandez cannot use. If he had, it would have torn the scene to pieces, and altered the course of the play. For the play's real intention, after all, is to say something about the integration struggle without saying anything about the root of it.

If you will examine the play carefully, you will find that the only really wicked people in the play are wicked because they are insane. They are covered, therefore, and the crimes of the republic are hidden. If we get rid of all these mad people, the play seems to be saying, "We'll get together and everything will be all right." The realities of economics, sex, politics, and history are thus swept under the rug.

Now the Negro actor, after all, is also a person and was not born two seconds before he enters the casting office. By the time he gets to that office, he has probably been an elevator boy, a cab driver, a dishwasher, a porter, a longshoreman. His blood is already thick with humiliations, and if he has any sense at all, he knows how small are his chances of making it in the theatre. He does a great deal of acting in the casting office, more, probably, than he will ever be allowed to do onstage. And, whatever his training, he is not there to get a role he really wants to play: he is there to get a role which will allow him to be seen.

It is all too likely that he has seen actors inferior to himself in training and talent rise far above him. And now, here he is, once more, facing an essentially ignorant and uncaring white man or woman, who *may* allow him to play a butler or a maid in the show being cast. He dissembles his experience in the office, and he knows that he will probably be lying about it onstage. He also knows why; it is because nobody wants to know the story. It would upset them. To begin analyzing all of his probable reactions, and the ways in which he reacts against his reactions, would take all of the space of this magazine, and then some. But resentment is compounded by the fact, as a Negro actress once observed to me, that not only does the white world impose the most intolerable conditions on Negro life, they also presume to dictate the mode, manner, terms, and style of one's reaction against these conditions.

Or, as a Negro playwright tells it, explaining how Ketti Frings came to adapt Richard Wright's *Long Dream* for the stage: "She was sitting by this swimming pool, see, and reading this book, and she thought, 'This would make a perfectly *darling* play.'

"So she wrote the first few scenes and called out her Negro butler, chauffeur, and maid, and read it to them and asked, 'Now, isn't that the way you poor, downtrodden, colored people feel about things?' 'Why, yes, Miss Frings,' they answered: and, I thought so, says the playwright—and so we go on. And on and on."

The point of this introductory column—for the readers of *The Urbanite* will be hearing a great deal from me—is that the theatre is perishing for the lack of vitality. Vitality, humanly and artistically speaking, has only one source, and that source is life. Now, the life actually being led on this continent is not the life which we pretend it is. White men are not what they take themselves to be, and Negroes are very different—to say the very least—from the popular image of them.

This image must be cracked, not only if we are to achieve a theatre—for we do not really have a theatre now, only a series of commercial speculations which result in mammoth musicals, and "daring" plays like *Compulsion* and *Inherit the Wind,* which are about as daring as a spayed tom-cat—this image must be cracked if we intend to survive as a nation. The Negro-in-America is increasingly the central problem in American life, and not merely in social terms, in personal terms as well.

I intend, from time to time, in discussing the theatre, to return to this point, for I think the time has come to begin a bloodless revolution. Only by a more truthful examination of what is really happening here can we realize the real aims of the theatre which are to instruct through terror and pity and delight and love. The only thing we can now do for the "tired business man" is to scare the living daylights out of him.

Both the Albee plays at the York Theatre—*The Death of Bessie Smith* and *The American Dream*—left me rather waiting for the other shoe to fall. Both plays seemed to promise more than they delivered; but I am not at all certain that I know what it is that they promised. This is not, by the way, meant as a complaint or as a joke. I don't mind—in the theatre, at any rate—having my cozy expectations swept out from under me; and I'm the type that enjoys being forced to ask myself just what the author had in mind. I was hardly ever moved "to the heart," as we say, by either of the Albee plays, but I *was* mystified, enraged, amused and horrified. I don't know if you will like them or not, but I think you ought to see them.

To take the plays in the order in which they were presented: *The Death of Bessie Smith* takes place in the Deep South, much of it in a thoroughly demoralizing hospital. There is not a single attractive person in this play, unless one excepts the off-stage Bessie

Smith, and the good-natured but simple-minded type who takes her on the journey which ends in her death.

Neither Bessie nor this man have much to do with the main action of the play. There is a question in my mind as to whether they really do much to illuminate it, but we will discuss this in a moment. In the course of the play, Bessie Smith dies off-stage and this is the extent, on the surface, anyway, of her connection with this drama.

The play's principal concern—I *think*—is with the character of a white Southern nurse. Character is perhaps not quite the word I want; rarely has less character been presented at greater or more unsympathetic length. I hesitate, possibly because I am a coward, to suppose that this creature is intended, in any way, to represent the fair ladies of the South. And yet, she is clearly of no interest in herself, except clinically; and I must add that, as I watched her, my own memories of Southern faces came flooding back, bringing with them the near-certainty that this horror, this emptiness, might very well be what the Southern face—and particularly the faces of the women— hide. I imagine that anyone who is old enough will not fail to be reminded of the faces and the personalities of the women who accused the Scottsboro boys of rape.

We first encounter this woman with her father—and they deserve each other—on the porch of their home. She is icily and methodically, and not for the first time—they certainly have nothing else to talk about—puncturing his delusions as to his person, his political ambitions, and his friendship with the Mayor, who is a patient in the hospital where she works on the admissions desk.

The relationship between the father and daughter is absolutely unspeakable, as are almost all the other relationships in this play; but I was puzzled as to what, precisely, Mr. Albee wished me to make of it. It is a relationship which, like the character of the nurse, is really of no interest in itself, it being doomed, by the lack of resources in the people, to be static. They will have this conversation over and over, then they will die, or the curtain will fall: and what either we or they have learned in the meantime is a question.

It may be that Mr. Albee's intention was to reveal, as forcefully as possible, the depth of the Southern poverty and paranoia, and the extent of the sexual ruin. But if this is so, then I think he has miscalculated.

I sympathize with him in the dilemma to which his raw material, his personages have drawn him. I am an Amercan writer, too, and

I know how it sets the teeth on edge to try to create, out of people clearly incapable of it—incapable of self-examination, of thought, or literally, of speech—drama that will reveal them. But the solution is not, to my mind, to present these people as they see themselves or *as they are;* we must be enabled to see them as they have been or as they might become; otherwise, we merely judge them as specimens and feel nothing for them as human beings.

It has, perhaps, never been more difficult than it is now to illuminate the person beleagured and bewildered by the irresponsibility and provincialism and worship of mediocrity which he, in his innocence, mistakes for democracy. On the other hand, it has possibly never been more important. So that I do not object to the deadly, hysterical stasis of the nurse, but to the fact that Mr. Albee never forces me to identify her inhumanity, her poverty, her terror, with my own.

For, in essence, the passionless brimstone exchanges which open the play *are* the play: the tone never changes, and we never learn very much more about the nurse, or the other people in the play, or about the community in which the action takes place. There is an arresting sequence between the nurse and a Negro orderly; but I must confess that the intention here was hopelessly muddled for me by the casting—I could not tell, at once, whether Harold Scott was playing a white man or a light Negro; and when it was clear that he was playing a Negro, I found myself distracted by the question of whether any Negro in the Deep South would so expose himself to this white witch. I did not know what to make of the interne, a dull type at best, it seemed to me; and whatever sympathy I might have been expected to feel for him was demolished by his incomprehensible passion to take the nurse to bed. (Whatever for?) This leaves, I believe, only the brief appearance of another, wonderfully distracted nurse, the off-stage Bessie, and her last paramour.

And here, again, either I have totally misunderstood Mr. Albee's intention, or he has miscalculated. I expected, at some point in the play, some ruthless flash which would illuminate the contrast between the wonderfully reckless life and terrible death of Bessie Smith and the whited sepulchre in which the nurse is writhing. But this does not happen. Bessie Smith bleeds to death, the nurse is the only character who knows who she is—earlier, her father had protested her addiction to 'nigger' music—and the nurse succumbs to hysteria. She announces that she, too, can sing and, horribly, tries.

I think I understand Mr. Albee's intention here, all right, but I think it fails of its effect: because there is no agony in it. People pay for the lives they lead and the crimes they commit and the blood-guiltiness from which they flee, whether they know they do or not. The effort not to know what one knows is the most corrupting effort one can make—which the nurse abundantly proves. But the anguish which comes when the buried knowledge begins to force itself to the light—which *must* be what is happening to the nurse upon the death of Bessie Smith—has driven countless thousands to madness or murder or grace, but certainly far beyond hysteria.

The American Dream turns out to be the gelded youth, so admired here and now. It presents a much more bland and amusing surface, but can scarcely qualify, obviously, as a funny play. Its vision of the antiseptic passivity of American life, and the resulting death of the masculine sensibility makes it more closely resemble a nightmare. I cannot synopsize this play, which offers even less in the way of story (and even more in the way of incident) than *Bessie Smith*. It begins at a marvelous clip, making its deadly observations with a salty, impertinent speed. ("I've got a right to all your money when you die," says Mommy to Daddy, "because I used to let you lie on top of me and bump your uglies." Daddy, needless to say, has long since given *that* up.) But it goes flat about half-way and finally surrenders much too quietly.

I came away with the feeling that it was a far better play than the author realized, and that he had given it up much too soon. Or that both these plays were exercises, notes for work which Mr. Albee has yet to do. I imagine that he will find it necessary to do much more violence to theatrical forms than he has so far done if he is to get his story told.

It is possible that what I am really complaining about here is a certain coldness, intrinsic to Albee, which will always mar his work. But I doubt this. For one thing, the venom which has gone into the portraits of the nurse in *Bessie Smith,* and the parents in *American Dream* does not argue too great a detachment, but too indignant a distaste. And he has a strange way with language, a beat which is entirely his, which may be controlled by the head, but which seems to be dictated from the guts.

Gwendolyn Brooks

(Mrs. Henry Blakely) of Chicago, has
won four Poetry Workshop Awards,
the *Mademoiselle* Merit Award; an
award by the Academy of Arts and
Letters; two Guggenheim Fellowships
and, among several other awards, the
Pulitzer Prize in Poetry. She includes
among her books *Poetry, The Bean
Eaters, Annie Allen, A Street in
Bronzeville,* a children's work and, in
fiction, *Maud Martha.*

Medgar Evers

The man whose height his fear improved he
arranged to fear no further. The raw
intoxicated time was time for better birth

or

a final death.
Old styles, old tempos, all the engagement of
the day—the sedate, the regulated fray—
the antique light, the Moral rose, old gusts,
tight whistlings from the past, the mothballs
in the Love at last our man forswore.
Medgar Evers annoyed confetti and assorted
brands of businessmen's eyes.
The shows came down: to maxims and surprise.
And palsy.
Roaring no rapt arise-ye to the dead he
Leaned across tomorrow. People said that
he was holding clean globes in his hands.

Junius Edwards

a Eugene F. Saxton Fellowship winner, 1959, was educated in Chicago
and the University of Oslo. Winner
of the Writer's Digest Short Story
Contest, 1958, Mr. Edwards' work has
appeared in the *Transatlantic Review*,
The Urbanite and other publications.
He is the author of the novel, *If We
Must Die*.

Mother dear and daddy

THEY CAME in the night while we slept. We knew they were coming, but not when, and we expected to see them when they did. We never thought that they would come at night. When we got up, well, when John, my brother, got up (he was always getting up early), when he got up, he looked out of the window and ran and jumped back in bed and shook me and called my name.

"Jim, Jim, they here. They here already. Wake up, Jim. They—"

"Hey, quit shaking me. I been woke long time."

"They here," he ran to the window. "Come on look."

He didn't have to tell me "come on look" because I was at the window when he got there, almost, anyway. They had come all right; we could see the cars parked in the yard, like big cats crouching, backs hunched, ready to attack.

"I'll go tell Mary, then," John said, and bolted out of the room as fast as you could blow out a coal oil lamp.

While he was out telling our three sisters, I stood there at the window and counted the cars. There were five in all, besides our car, and they were all black and shiny as my plate whenever I got through eating red beans and rice. Our car sat over there by itself, dusty and dirty as one of those bums that come by all the time wanting a meal.

I stood there, leaning on the windowsill, with my right foot on top of my left foot, scratching my left foot with my toes, and looking at our car. I could feel my eyes burning, burning, and the tears coming and washing the burns, and me sucking my tongue because of the burning and trying not to make a sound. My body went cold and inside it I could feel something surging up; not like being sick, this surging came up my whole body, my arms, too, and ended with my eyes burning. I fought to hold it back, keep it buried. Even when I was alone, I always fought it, always won and kept it down, even at times when it was sudden and fast and got to my eyes and burned like hot needles behind my eyelids, hot needles with legs running around trying to get past my eyelids and spill out on my cheeks, even then I kept it down.

I had fought it for two weeks and I was good at it and getting better. Maybe I was good at it because of that first day. I had not fought it then. I had let it come, right in front of Aunt Mabel, I let it come, not trying to stop it, control it; I let it come.

"What we going to do?" I asked Aunt Mabel, after it had come, had shaken me and left me as empty as an unfilled grave. "What we going to do, Aunt Mabel?"

"Lord knows, son. Lord knows," Aunt Mabel said, sitting in her rocker, moving, slow, back and forth, looking down at me, on my knees, my arms resting on her huge right thigh and my head turned up to her, watching that round face, her lips tight now, her head shaking side to side, and her eyes clouded, and me not understanding her answer, but thinking I should and not daring to ask again and feeling the question pounding my brain: What we going to do? What we going to do?

"The Lord giveth and the Lord taketh away."

But, what we going to do? I could not understand Aunt Mabel. I did not know what her mumbling about The Lord had to do with this. All I knew was she had just told me Mother Dear and Daddy were dead. Mother Dear and Daddy were dead. Mother Dear and Daddy would not come back. Mother Dear and Daddy wouldn't take us home again. What we going to do?

"I want to go home. I want to go home," I screamed and got to my feet and ran to the door, realizing it was Aunt Mabel calling my name. I ran out to the yard where John and our sisters played, and right past them. I did not feel my feet move; I did not feel I owned a body. I wanted to get home. And hearing Aunt Mabel call my name, seeing houses, cars, people, trees, like one big thing made of windows, walls, wheels, heads, branches, arms and legs and behind that one big thing, our house, with our car out front, and our yard and our tree, and then the big thing was gone and I was at our house, running up the steps across the porch, as fast as I could, straight to the screened door, wham! and I lay on my back on the porch looking up at the screen, at the imprints made in it by my head and hands and my right knee. I got right up and started banging on the door, trying to twist the knob.

"Mother Dear! Daddy! Mother Dear! Daddy!" I called as loud as I could and kept banging on the door. Then, I ran to the back door and called again and banged and kicked the door. They did not come.

They would not come.

"Mother Dear! Daddy! It's me. Let me in. Open the door!"

They would not come.

I ran to the front, out to the street and turned and looked up to their room and saw the shades were drawn just as they were drawn when Mother Dear and Daddy took us over to Aunt Mabel's house to stay for the weekend while they went away fishing with cousin Bob.

I cupped my hands up to my mouth.

"Mother Dear. Daddy. Mother Dear! Daddy!"

I called, and called again and all the while I kept my eyes glued on that window, waiting. Any moment now, any second now, now, *now*, waited to see that white shade zoom up and then the window, and then Mother Dear and Daddy, both together, lean out, smiling, laughing, waving, calling my name, now, now, *now*.

They did not come.

They would not come. The shade stood still, stayed still, with the sun shining on it through the window pane; stayed still, as if the sun were a huge nail shooting through the pane and holding it down. It did not go up. It would not go up.

They would not come.

I knew it. Suddenly, just like that, snap, I knew they would not come; could not come. The shades would stay still. I knew they would not come. I lowered my hands, my eyes darting from shaded window to shaded window, around the yard, under the house, searching, for what? I did not know, and then there was the car. My eyes were glued to the car, and I started over to it, slowly at first, and then I ran and I stopped short and pressed my head up against the glass in the front door beside the steering wheel. The glass was hot on my nose and lips and forehead, and burned them, but I did not care, I pressed harder, as if by doing so I could push right through the glass, not breaking it, but melting through it. Then, I felt as though I *was* inside, in my favorite spot up front with Daddy, and in back were Mother Dear and John and our sisters; Daddy whistling and the trees going by and the farms and green, green, green, and other cars and Daddy starting to sing and all of us joining him singing "Choo-choo Train to Town," even Jo Ann and Willie Mae, who had not learned the words yet, singing, singing, and ending laughing and feeling Daddy's hand on my head.

"Jim." I turned from the window, and it was Aunt Mabel's hand on my head.

"Come on, son." She took my right hand and led me up the street as if I were a baby just starting to walk.

"What we going to do, Aunt Mabel?"

"You got to be brave, Jim. You the oldest. You got to look out for your brother and sisters."

I decided then that I would not let my brother and sisters see me cry, ever. I was twelve years old and the oldest and I had to take care of them.

"When can we go back home, Aunt Mabel?"

"I guess we ought to move over to your house while we wait for the family to get here," Aunt Mabel said. "It's bigger than mine and your clothes there."

I looked up at Aunt Mabel. I had not expected her to move back with us. I wanted only we children to move back home.

When we got back to Aunt Mabel's house I told John about the automobile accident and that Mother Dear and Daddy were dead. John was only eight, but he understood and he cried and I understood just how he felt, so I left him alone.

The next day we moved back to our house. Aunt Mabel, too. Every time one of our sisters would ask for Mother Dear and Daddy we always said they were gone away. They were too young to understand about death.

Aunt Mabel told me that our Uncles and Aunts and Grandparents were coming. I didn't know any of them. I remembered Christmas presents from them and Mother Dear and Daddy talking about them, but I had never seen them.

"They're good folks," Aunt Mabel said, "and it won't make no difference which one you all go to live with."

"But, Aunt Mabel. We going to stay home."

"You can't son. You all too young to stay here by yourself and I can't take care of you."

"I can take care of us, Aunt Mabel. I'm the oldest. I can take care of us."

Aunt Mabel smiled. "Bet you could, too. But you all need somebody to be a Mamma and a Papa to you. You all got to go live with one of your Aunts and Uncles."

I knew right away that Aunt Mabel was right. I told John about it and we started trying to guess where we would go. The family was scattered all over, mostly in big cities like New York, Philadelphia and Boston. Our Grandfather on Daddy's side was in Texas. John and I couldn't decide what we liked best: Texas and horses or big cities and buildings. We talked about it every day while we waited for them to come, and now they were here.

I left the window and started to get dressed. John ran back into the room.

"Them won't wake up."

"They can sleep, then," I said. "Let's go see where the cars came from."

We got dressed and ran out to the yard and looked at the license plates. There were two from New York, two from Pennsylvania and one from Massachusetts.

"None of them from Texas," I said.

"Which one you like best?" asked John.

"That one," I said, pointing to the one from Massachusetts. I liked it because it was the biggest one. The five of us could get in it without any trouble at all.

We examined each car carefully for an hour and then Aunt Mabel called us and told us to come in the house.

"They all here," she said, "all that's coming, I guess. Now, you all be good so they'll like you."

I followed Aunt Mabel into the living room. I could feel John right behind me, up close, and I could hear his breathing.

"Here the boys," Aunt Mabel announced, and walked across the room and sat down.

John and I stopped at the door. Our sisters were lined up, side by side, in the middle of the room, smiling. I had heard voices before we came into the room, but now, there was silence and all eyes were on us. They sat in a half circle in straight back chairs, near the walls around the room. I looked at them. I stared at each face. Aunt Mabel and our sisters were the only smiling faces I saw. I didn't know about John, but right at that moment, I was scared. I wanted to turn and run away as fast as I could. I felt as if I had committed the worst crime and those faces hated me for it. Besides Aunt Mabel, there were five men and five women, all dressed in black. Each man had a black line above his upper lip. The two men who were fat had thick black lines and the other three had thinner ones. I didn't like the lines. Daddy never wore one and I always thought his face was cleaner and friendlier and happier than other men I had seen who wore them.

I noticed the features of these people right away. They were all like Mother Dear, Aunt Mabel and our sisters, and they were pink rose. I knew they were Mother Dear's relatives. Daddy didn't have any brothers or sisters and he used to tell John and me whenever we got into a fight with each other that we should be kind to each other because we were brothers and it was good to have a brother and that he wished he had had brothers and sisters. Mother Dear had plenty of brothers and sisters. She had three brothers, and I knew them right away as the three who weren't fat, and three sisters, Aunt Mabel, of course, and the two women who sat beside the fat men.

I stood there looking, staring at those faces that looked as if they had just taken straight castor oil. I looked at John, now standing at my right. He stood there with his mouth hanging open and his eyes straight ahead. I could tell he was scared and as soon as I knew he was scared, I wasn't scared any more and I wanted to tell him not to be scared because I wasn't going to let anything happen to him. Just when I was about to tell him, Aunt Mabel broke the silence.

"Come on over here next to your sisters," she said.

We shuffled over to where our sisters were and stood there like slaves on auction.

"They good children," Aunt Mabel said. "No trouble at all."

The others still kept quiet, except for whispers among themselves.

"Say your names, boys," Aunt Mabel said.

"James," I said.

"John," said John.

"We call James, Jim," Aunt Mabel said, and smiled at me.

I looked at her. It was all right for her to call me Jim. Mother Dear and Daddy called me Jim. I looked back at those faces. I didn't want *them* to call me Jim.

"Well," Aunt Mabel said to them, "You all going to tell the boys your names?"

They introduced themselves to us, not smiling, not changing those castor oil expressions. Apparently they had already introduced themselves to our sisters.

"Mabel," one of the fat men said, "why don't you get these kids out of here so we can talk."

"Jim, you and the children go in the dining room," Aunt Mabel said, and when we were going, she added, "And close the door."

We went into the dining room and I closed the door. Our sisters sat down in the middle of the floor and played. John stood over them, watching, but when he saw me with my ear to the door, he came over and joined me. We faced each other with our heads pressed up against the door and we listened. The only voice I could recognize was Aunt Mabel's.

"Carol and I have thought this thing over and we can see our way clear to take the girls," one of the men said.

"Now, wait a minute, Sam," another woman said. "We thought we'd take *one* of the girls, at least."

Then, for a minute it sounded as if they were all trying to get a word in. They talked all at the same time, even yelled. It sounded as if everyone wanted a girl.

"Lord have mercy. You mean you going to split them up? You mean they won't be together?"

"Five kids? Frankly, we can't afford two, but we'd be willing to take the three girls."

There was another minute of all of them trying to speak at the same time, at the top of their voices, each one wanting a girl.

"Why don't you all talk like people? I don't like to see them split up, but I guess five is too many for anybody, specially when they not your own."

"Then you understand that they'll have to be separated? There's no other way, and since we already have a son, we thought we would take one of the girls."

"Well," Aunt Mabel said, "look like to me all you all want a girl. I didn't hear nobody say nothing about the boys, yet."

There was silence. John and I pressed harder against the door. John's mouth was open, his bottom lip hanging, and he was staring at me hard. I could tell he was scared and I must have looked scared to him so I closed my own mouth and tried to swallow. There was nothing to swallow and I had to open my mouth again and take a deep breath.

"Come to think of it, you all didn't say one word to them boys," Aunt Mabel said. "Why don't you all want boys?"

"We have a boy."

"We do, too."

"Girls are easier."

"Boys are impossible."

"Lord have mercy."

"Listen, Mabel, you don't understand the situation."

"Don't get on your high horse with me. Talk plain."

"All right, Mabel. The fact is, the boys are—well—they're too, well, too much like the father."

"What?"

"You heard me. I know that's why *we* don't want one, and it's probably why the others here don't want one and it's no use avoiding it."

"Is that right? Is that why you all don't want one, too?" Aunt Mabel asked.

There was silence.

"Lord have mercy. I never head such a thing in all my life. Your own sister's children, too."

"You don't understand, Mabel."

"No, I don't. Lord knows I don't. What you all doing up there? Passing? Huh? That what you doing? No. No. You couldn't be doing that. Even if you wanted to, you couldn't be doing that. You not that light that you can pass, none of you all. Lord have mercy. They too black for you. Your own sister's children."

John looked down at his hands, at the back of his hands and then at me and down at our sisters and at his hands again.

"I never thought I'd live to see the day my own flesh and blood would talk like that, and all the trouble in the world. My own sisters and brothers," Aunt Mabel said.

"Mabel, you've been here in this town all your life. This town isn't the world. You don't know how it is."

John rubbed the back of his hand on his pants and looked at it again.

I kept listening.

"It's hard enough like it is without having these boys, having to always explain about them. You can see that, Mabel. Look at us, how light we are. We'd always have to explain to everyone they're our dead sisters' boys and people who we don't explain to will jump to all kinds of conclusions. Socially, we'd be out, too. No, Mabel. That's just the way it is and we can't do a thing about it. I, for one, have certain standards I want to live up to and having these boys won't help.

"I never thought it. I never thought it."

"That's the way it is, Mabel. Those boys will do none of us any good."

John went over to where our sisters played and stood over them, examining them.

Aunt Mabel said: "So that's how come you didn't want her to get married. That's how come you tried to get her away from here."

John kneeled down and touched each one of our sisters. He looked at them and at his hand, at them and at his hand, and then to me. Then, his eyes became shiny and he started batting his eyes and the sides of his face grew, his cheeks puffed way out, his mouth closed tight. He fought it all he could and I knew it was useless, he would not succeed. I could feel the same thing happening to me, but I held it back and concentrated on him, watched his swelling face until it exploded and thinking he might yell out, I rushed to him and got down on my knees and held him, held him close, just as Daddy would have, with my left arm around his back and my right hand behind his head, holding his head to my chest and felt his body shaking like a balloon when you let out the air and I listened to him groan like a whipped dog. I didn't say one word to him. I couldn't. I let him cry and I held him and watched our sisters and they suddenly realized he was crying and they came to us and helped me hold him and tried to get him to tell why he cried and when he would not tell they asked me and when I would not tell they stood there holding both of us until John got control of himself. He sat back on his heels and sobbed and the girls stepped back and watched him. I stood up and watched all of them. The girls stood there and watched him and waited, their faces alert, ready to run to him and help him. It was as if they knew, now, this was not a physical wound that made him cry, not a twisted arm, a stubbed toe, or a beating, and certainly not a cry that would make them laugh and yell "cry baby" at him. It was as if they knew it was a wound they had never had and that it was deeper than skin.

I heard the voices in the living room, louder now, and wilder, so I started back to my place at the door, but before I got there, John lost control again. We got to him at the same time and tried to hold him, but this time he pushed us away, fought us off, and got to his feet and ran into the living room. I got to my feet as fast as I could and ran after him into the living room. He was screaming now and when I ran into the living room, I stopped short at what I saw. John had run in and jumped in the lap of the first man he came to and he was there on his knees in the man's lap screaming and pounding the man's chest and face. The man pushed him off and John fell to the floor on his back and got right up and jumped in the man's lap again, still screaming, and pounded the man's chest and face with both his little fists.

"John, John, John!" I yelled, and ran to him and pulled him out of the man's lap, just in time, too, because the man swung at him back handed, but I had John down and the man missed. John, still screaming, kicking, struggled with me, trying to get away from me so he could get back to the man.

"John, John!" I yelled, shaking him, trying to make him hear me. "John, John!", but I could see he wasn't listening to me even though he was looking straight at me as I stood in front of him holding both of his arms and shouting his name. He only screamed.

Suddenly, I started walking backwards from him, holding his arms still, pulling him along with me until we were in the center of the room and then I smiled at him. "Come on, John, come on, John," I said, and laughed, laughed hard, looking into his eyes, I kept it up, laughed loud and harder still and felt my body shake from it. Then I saw John's face change, first a smile, then he broke into a laugh, too. I stared into his eyes and we laughed. We laughed. We laughed. We laughed. We threw our heads back and we laughed. We held each other's hands and danced round and round and laughed. Our sisters came and joined our dance. We formed a circle, all of us laughing, laughing, and we danced round and round. We were the only people in the world. We danced round and round and laughed and laughed.

"Hey," I said, "Choo-Choo Train, Choo-Choo Train" and they joined me:

"Choo-choo train, choo-choo train
We going to take that choo-choo train
Choo-choo train to town
Choo-choo train
Choo-choo train"

Round and round, "Choo-choo train" louder and louder I sang, "CHOO-CHOO TRAIN, CHOO-CHOO TRAIN, CHOO-CHOO TRAIN TO TEXAS" round and round "CHOO-CHOO TRAIN" until I realized what I had said and I screamed happily and said it again and again until they caught on and said it, too. We went faster and faster and said it louder and louder sounding like a Choo-choo Train: TEXAS, TEXAS, TEXAS, TEXAS, TEXAS . . . .

Hoyt W. Fuller

is the editor of the *Negro Digest* in
Chicago. His publications in the literary magazines are many; his activities on the Chicago book scene are
varied and indefatigable. Mr. Fuller
is said to be by many critics among
the most unsung, but most knowl-
edgeable book men in the U.S. He
has travelled widely in Europe and
Africa and in 1965 won a Whitney
Fellowship.

The apostle

AS CLYDE HEDGER wheeled his Chevrolet sedan onto the expressway and sped southward in the stream of morning traffic, he felt
downright gay. The project on which he was embarking was so
simple—even *natural*—that it now seemed incredible he had never
thought of it before. He was driving across town for an appointment
with the famous ("Infamous, really," he chuckled to himself) Apostle,
an interview which might very well prove the key to his advancement
to a vice presidency of Keene and Associates Advertising Company,
Inc. At twenty-eight, and after only three years as a junior executive
at the firm, Mr. Hedger already stood at the very portals of that
high-ranking post, and only a brilliant stroke like signing the Apostle
was needed to bring it off. It was no secret at the agency that Mr.
Keene, deeply enmeshed in emotional and litigious involvements with
two beautiful women, one of them his wife, leaned with increasing
weariness on the sturdier shoulders of the more singular-minded Mr.
Hedger. And Mr. Hedger more than justified this reliance with new
accounts and spectacular production. Within the past few months,
for instance, he had conceived and directed a project for Summit
Meat Products which had almost doubled that firm's city-wide sales.
He had accomplished this by persuading two public idols—the star
catcher of the city's baseball team and the city's most popular disc
jockey—to endorse Summit meats. With some 700,000 or 800,000
Negroes in the city (nobody seemed to be able to come up with a
more exact number) still to be directly influenced, corraling the
Apostle was not merely an opportunity, it was a duty. That the man
was an outright charlatan was beside the point. After all, he wasn't
supporting the man; he was merely going to exploit him, for a price,
just as he had the ballplayer and the disc jockey. Smiling roguishly,
Mr. Hedger recalled his secretary's sarcastic summation of the Apostle
and his cult. "The Apostle's secretary says he has over a million followers all over, but was rather vague about the number locally,"
Miss Henderson had droned. "The church, she says, holds over a
thousand, and it's always full. As a round figure for local followers,
she gave two hundred thousand. Inflation, of course. They don't

keep a membership list, only of disciples. Disciples, sometimes called 'lambs,' are inner-circle cultists, and they number about ten thousand. All round numbers, you see. That gal had it down like a circus spieler, and it all sounds like hokum." Old Dora and her prejudices, Mr. Hedger thought cheerily. Well, all he cared about was that—when the Apostle spoke—the South Side listened.

The idea of signing up the Apostle had come to him suddenly Sunday afternoon, three days earlier. He and Janice were lounging around the living room, as they usually did on Sundays, and he was still thumbing through the papers. Jan was beginning to grow restless, having finished the society and entertainment sections, the only pages that interested her. She flipped on the television control, remarking with no particular enthusiasm that there was an old Marilyn Monroe movie on, and then she flopped down beside him. Neither of them had bothered to change the dial, or the volume, and the face and voice which flared forth from the screen were worlds away from the sexy movie star.

Mr. Hedger laughed out loud recalling the shock on his wife's pretty face. She actually went bone-white. There filling the twenty-three inch screen was the slate-black, swollen featured face, fantastically crowned, of a ranting Negro, his pit-deep voice so loud that it shook the apartment. Janice Hedger physically recoiled, her hands automatically flew to her face. Well, to be honest, Mr. Hedger admitted that he also momentarily froze at the sight.

The face was wet with sweat and, in the heat and glare of klieg lights, glittered like moonlit water. The eyes were small and bulbous, the eyebrows wispy, but the nose and lips, spread across the broad face, were as emphatically sculptured as cast-iron. An embroidered white turban arched over the brow and rose into the unseen beyond the borders of the screen. ". . . I will show you the way to salvation, my lambs," the great plowing voice promised. "I am the Apostle. Follow me. The Kingdom of Heaven has a training ground here on earth, and it is here, right here in this very building, this temple of the Divine Supremacy . . ."

By this time Mrs. Hedger had recovered equilibrium enough to stalk across the room and switch the dial. "Holy Moses!" she said, adjusting the sound to normal room volume. "What a monster!" But Mr. Hedger's agile mind was dancing. There were all those stories and jokes about the Apostle. It was said that the man performed black magic, that he conjured up apparitions, that he sold lottery numbers and seduced wealthy old widows. He had a fleet of Cadillacs, a couple dozen servants in livery, enough furs and finery to outfit a harem, more jewelry than Babs Hutton . . . Mr. Hedger recalled the night, months earlier, he had driven through the South Side on the way to visit his parents in the suburbs. Approaching the old Apollo Theatre he had noticed mobs of Negroes under the marquee and spilling over into the street. The red flashers of police cars enflamed the sky, and the officers scurried around on foot trying to keep the street open to traffic. He had asked one of the officers, a tall, prize-fighter type who reminded him of the young Joe Louis, what was going on at the theatre. "That's not a theatre anymore, mister, that's the Apostle's church," the policeman told him. "There's a near-riot here everytime the doors open. Everybody wants to get inside." Glancing up at the marquee, Mr. Hedger had noted that, indeed, the words "The Apostle" gleamed where "Apollo" had once been.

Mr. Hedger's blossoming scheme demanded that he retrieve the lost program and, against his wife's protests, he switched the dial back to the Apostle. "This character is going to mean money in the bank for us." It was an irresistible argument. Mrs. Hedger cuddled up beside her husband and was quiet.

". . . We have such great strength, and we waste it," the Apostle said. He spoke in a sorghumy, insinuating tone which—like an intra-racial attic—seemed stored with old and bitter memories. "We have such wonderful power, and we fritter it away. Children, I tell you, my lambs, we have such unheard of wealth, and we are poor. I will show you how to be strong, my lambs. I will show you how to use your power. I will show you how to be truly rich . . ." He beamed a benevolently monarchial smile, raised a flared sleeve into camera range and mopped his black face with a huge white handkerchief. He shook his head and rumbled, "Ah, yes, it's true, my lambs," and flashed the kingly smile. "My lambs, my children, there is so much evil around us, it's everywhere you turn. Evil people. You must fight this evil. Come to me and I will show you how. I am with you. You people out there in the television audience, I come to you because our glorious temple is just not big enough to accommodate everybody. Then, too, so many of you have requested to visit me privately, but there is room for only a few at a time at my little place. Paradise, my little home. And I must have rest. So, you understand, my lambs, if I can't see you all. And it's expensive, my lambs, to bring you this television message of your salvation. You can help me do it. Will you help me? For I must fight evil. Evil is ugly, and I don't like ugly. God don't like ugly, and the Apostle don't like ugly, my lambs. Remember that. I don't like ugly, I just don't like ugly . . . ."

On that repetitive refrain, the sound gradually diminished until the hypnotic voice was inaudible. The cameras simultaneously retreated from the Apostle's face, drawing away until his full figure was visible in the center of a stage. He wore a gorgeous gown of bright shimmering material which swept the floor. Behind him, arrayed over the width of the stage against a curtain backdrop, stood a robed choir of dark-faced men and women. The Apostle raised an arm and, abruptly, the chorus filled the theater with rousing jazz-beat song. Again the sound faded, and the scene shifted to the television studios, focusing on the white, cinematically serene face of an announcer. The man's cool, measured tone pealed into the room like chimes on the tail of a dirge. Mrs. Hedger said, "What a phony!" in obvious relief, but Mr. Hedger's attention remained fastened on the screen. The announcer said, "The preceding telecast was a presentation of the Commonwealth of the Triumph of the Divine Supremacy," a smirk crowding the edges of his professionally poker expression.

It was Mrs. Hedger who turned the set off. "Now I believe all I've ever heard about that guy," she said in disgust.

Mr. Hedger remained pensive. "He's a big man on the South Side, Jan. Thousands of followers. They'll do anything he says."

"It's frightening!"

"No, you don't understand." Mr. Hedger began to display his excitement. "It's a great opportunity. Look, all the Apostle's followers eat meat. With the Apostle telling them to buy Summit, the factory won't be able to make the stuff fast enough!"

Mrs. Hedger murmured something about the Apostle taking advantage of ignorant people and prating about salvation, but Mr. Hedger emphasized the man's power. "He can elect the mayor, Jan," he said. She was unimpressed. "He kept saying, 'I don't like ugly, I don't like ugly,' as if he never looked in a mirror. Why, he's ugly enough to shut down a clock factory." Mr. Hedger ignored her. "We can confine the campaign to the South Side, use throw-aways, billboards and ads in the Negro papers," he said. "It will be a breeze."

Miss Henderson, the secretary Mr. Hedger had inherited from Mr. Keene and on whom he depended for seasoned advice, had seen the immediate possibilities of his plan. She proceeded to quote statistics relative to the Negro market ("Negroes in this country have a bigger annual income than the whole of Canada. Just imagine that! And they have the gall to complain about conditions.") and to warn against the pitfalls of religion ("With this Apostle fellow there might be problems. You have to be so careful with these sects and cults, honey."). Miss Henderson obviously was not fond of Negroes and never hesitated to say so ("They're as slippery as eels, honey"), and she did not hesitate now. "Personally, I wouldn't go near the critter for any amount of money, but it's your funeral, honey," she said. Mr. Hedger resented facile expressions of racism and considered challenging Miss Henderson's remarks, but he settled for a mild, "And why not, Dora, what's so different about him?" Mr. Hedger sometimes, as a moral duty, lectured to skeptical friends about their racial prejudices. Negroes are like anybody else, he would tell them. It gave him a sense of maturity and authority to be able to isolate and squelch racial myths. After all, he knew from experience. He had sat in classes with Negroes in college and bunked next to them in the Army. However, he was in too light-hearted a mood for arguing now, so he settled for some ungallant observations of Miss Henderson. Wrinkles showed through the heavy make-up on her long face, he noted, and her dyed red hair, pulled back from her face like a mane, gave her the appearance of a rouged horse. He wondered whatever had attracted Mr. Keene to the woman in the first place. Mr. Hedger gave Miss Henderson a bland little smile and asked her to get background information on the Apostle and the Commonwealth of the Triumph of the Divine Supremacy, plus Negro population figures. He needed the facts for presentation to Mr. Keene. She promised a report within the hour, and Mr. Hedger knew she would have it. Dora Henderson *was* efficient. "I just hope you can handle the coon," she said as she opened the door to leave. Mr. Hedger drily told her he could.

The entire project was all but wrapped up that very morning. Mr. Keene, as expected, approved the plan, and a call to Dave Koscinski at Summit brought enthusiastic support. "We've been thinking about moving out in the Black Belt for some time," Mr. Koscinski said. "We do pretty well out there as it is, but naturally we can do a lot better. Those people eat more meat than we do, you know. Especially pork. They thrive on it. So go right ahead, Clyde. Summit is one hundred percent behind you." A little later, Miss Henderson announced that the Apostle had agreed to receive Mr. Hedger at nine-thirty Wednesday morning. Mr. Hedger was so pleased with himself that he felt like lighting up a cigar but, having none available, he settled for a cigarette. Things couldn't have been going better.

As he turned his car up the ramp leading of the expressway, Mr. Hedger hummed merrily. He checked his notes for the Apostle's address and headed for the street. The Apostle's Paradise was situated in a part of the city rarely visited by Mr. Hedger. The neighborhood once had been elegant, inhabited by some of the state's richest and most highly placed people. As a child, he often had driven with his parents along the wide boulevards, marvelling at the landscaped gardens and wondering about the life behind the forbidding walls. But the neighborhood in recent years had been a battle-ground in the seemingly interminable racial war of living areas. In this warfare, it was the pattern of conflict that Negroes were the aggressors, constantly storming and over-running the bastions of the embattled whites. As the whites withdrew, establishing new positions behind new Maginot lines, the Negroes spilled over into the freshly evacuated territory, pausing only to solidify their occupation before plunging forth in the next assault. The Apostle had been in the vanguard of this army of occupation, and his billet, the three-story graystone Soderheim mansion (thirty rooms, indoor swimming pool, gymnasium), was a truly worthy spoil. Mr. Hedger, having imagined in the ankle regions of his mind that the Apostle's place of residence would match his flamboyant television image (possibly with neon signs announcing "This is Paradise"), was mildly disappointed to find the mansion virtually as staid as in its more respectable past. There was a touch of individuality in the vertical blinds at the front windows and in the blue and white striped awning over the stoop, but these girlish additions to the dowager building were less than sensational.

Mr. Hedger arrived at the mansion at nine-twenty and, finding no parking space in the block, double-parked in front of the sprawling lawn. Someone was sure to emerge from one of the surrounding buildings and move a car. He surveyed the block. On both sides of the boulevard the houses sat rods from the street, the doorways reached by cement walks that wound over grounds once uniformly green and manicured but now mostly pocked and scabbed like mangy hides. Some of the buildings towered four stories, as tall as apartment buildings which most, in fact, had become. There were tales that many of the high-ceilinged old bedrooms now housed whole families, and this, Mr. Hedger concluded, accounted for the bumper-to-bumper crop of cars at the curbs.

Two middle-aged, comfortably heavy Negro women, dressed in smock-like dresses, approached on the sidewalk. One of them, brown, comely, with a sly, motherly face suggesting a roguish madonna, stopped suddenly, threw her head back and laughed lustily. The other woman, darker and more gentle, regaled her with some delicious story. A third woman walked toward them. Though the approximate age of the morning gossipers, this one was their opposite in appearance. She was corseted to slimness and impeccably dressed. She walked rapidly, head high, her narrow high heels tapping the pavement. As she passed the two women, she smiled an impersonal apology and stepped off the sidewalk onto the Apostle's lawn to avoid brushing the woman nearest her. The gossipers stopped talking, fixed their attention on the passing woman and glared at her. The darker woman made a mocking face, tossed her head and pranced like a clumsy drayhorse. Her friend howled uproariously at this performance, slapping the actress on the back like a logger in a barroom.

The laughter was infectious and Mr. Hedger found himself chuckling. Then he glanced at his watch and grew panicky. It was past nine-thirty. A motor turned over behind him, and he saw that the well-dressed Negro woman was at the wheel of the Cadillac at the curb. She adroitly maneuvered the big car into the street and, as she drove past Mr. Hedger, smiled warmly at him. Mr. Hedger gratefully smiled back, then hurriedly deposited his car in the vacated space.

Hugging his briefcase under his arm, Mr. Hedger hustled up the S-shaped walk to the canopied doorway and rang the bell. The door was opened immediately by a small, wiry man the color of brandy, wearing a royal blue uniform replete with brass buttons and a broad snaggle-toothed grin. He had an open, small-featured face that reflected all the hazards of some fifty years of living. "Good morning, sir," he said, his voice redolent of cotton fields and drafty cabins. "Can I help you, sir?"

"I have an appointment with the . . . with . . . with Mr. Apostle." The realization that he did not know the appropriate manner of addressing the Apostle brought Mr. Hedger a moment of alarm. The doorman, bowing, invited Mr. Hedger into a reception hall furnished with delicate, velvet-cushioned chairs that looked ancient and unused and ornate Oriental vases almost as tall as the doorman. Across a hallway a wide, richly carpeted stairway curved upwards. The doorman lifted a telephone from the table beside him. "What is the name, sir?"

"Hedger. Mr. Clyde Hedger of Keene and Associates."

"Yessir."

He dialed a number and, when a voice answered, announced, "Mr. Hedger to see His Goodness."

Mr. Hedger stiffened. Was he expected to call the man "His Goodness"?

"Yes, mam, Miss Shell, I'll send him right in." The doorman replaced the telephone and clicked on his jigsaw smile. "His Goodness will see you now, sir." He stepped into the areaway and pointed a bony finger. "At the end of the hall, sir. Miss Shell will take you in. Last room down the hall."

Mr. Hedger started off, then hesitated. "Excuse me, but how is the Apostle usually addressed by visitors?"

"Well, we lambs of the Commonwealth always call him His Goodness, but other folks usually just say Apostle Lovett. Just Apostle Lovett, sir."

"Thank you very much," Mr. Hedger said. "I never met Apostle Lovett before, and I wanted to be sure."

"Yessir, Apostle Lovett will be allright, sir."

"Thank you."

"A pleasure, sir."

Mr. Hedger strode down the padded and dark-paneled hallway. Having suppressed the impulse to add "lamb" to his "thank you," he now steadied himself for business by recalling data about the Apostle and his sect. "The Commonwealth of . . ." He stopped, found Miss Henderson's memo in his pocket and checked it. "Real name: Jesse Lovett. Cult: Commonwealth of the Triumph of the Divine Supremacy. Place of worship: Temple of the Divine Supremacy. Home: Paradise ('Hallelujah!' Miss Henderson had interpolated). Marital status: Uncertain, don't mention . . ."

Conscious of a presence, Mr. Hedger looked up. The dorway was open in front of him and a slim, youthful figure filled it. When his eyes lifted to her face he saw that she was as young and as comely as her figure and that she was smiling at him. She had curly black hair, worn like a tiara, green-gray eyes, lips that were full and very red, and skin the color of gold. Mr. Hedger slipped the memo in his pocket and uttered an embarrassed "Good morning." He decided that Miss Shell looked more like a night club hostess than a preacher's Girl Friday. "Good morning, Mr. Hedger," she said smokily. "Please come in."

He walked past her into an ante-chamber furnished with desk and typewriter, telephone, filing cabinet, chair and small leather couch. A wide window overlooked a garden, and a breeze from it wafted Miss Shell's perfume into Mr. Hedger's nostrils. He followed her into the adjoining room.

There he almost gasped in astonishment. He had visualized the Apostle surrounded by plush and gilt and outrageously luxurious trappings. Instead, the ballroom-sized room was practically bare. A magnificent window at the rear, its heavy wine-colored draperies half-drawn, admitted a rectangle of light into the otherwise unlighted vastness. The shaft of light fell across a desk no bigger nor handsomer than Miss Shell's and on an ordinary looking leather desk chair behind it. At an angle to the desk, just out of the light, was a leather lounge chair, apparently reserved for visitors. The room, like the hallway, was completely paneled in dark wood and the floor covered by a thick carpet of burnished burgundy. It seemed to Mr. Hedger, under the circumstances, as perversely austere as a monk's cell.

But if the room was a surprise, the man Mr. Hedger found there was a shock. It was hardly the same man he had seen on television. That man had been homely, yes, but with a certain attractiveness in his flaring features and deep, resonant voice. He had seemed as tall and as masterful as a Watussi prince in the dramatic headpiece and the flowing robe. But the man who met Mr. Hedger in the center of the great room now was remarkable only for his surpassing ugliness. The Apostle stood just over five feet and was shaped like an egg. His rough ebony skin seemed as tough as a crocodile's hide, and that portion of his head that had hidden under the turban was absolutely bald and glittered like polished glass. The nose and mouth which had seemed heroic on the screen seemed in person only grossly distorted. He extended a hand, grinning up at his visitor like a well-tailored but over-fed pygmy. "Good morning, Mr. Hedger."

Mr. Hedger realized, as he shook hands, that not even the Apostle's voice was the same. The under-plowing, Robesonian quality was there, sounding incongruous now in such an unimpressive person, but the intraracial, honey-slow, gospel-and-blues accent was gone. "It's a pleasure to have you here," the Apostle said, his diction as precise as a British don's. "Please come and sit down."

Mr. Hedger followed the Apostle to the desk and, after the cultist was seated, settled in the lounge chair. Then he saw that the Apostle, framed like some gnomish deity in the window light, looked down on him from behind the desk. The Apostle now seemed fully two heads taller than he had been standing, and Mr. Hedger decided that the Apostle's chair was not so ordinary after all. It did better than equalize the Apostle's height: it was raised to give him an advantage. And it was impossible not to look up to him. There was nothing else on which to focus attention. The Apostle sat primly, the welcoming grin unchanged on his face.

"I want to apologize for being late, Apostle Lovett," Mr. Hedger began. "I had a little trouble finding a parking space outside."

"Yes, we have quite a parking problem on our street," the basso voice replied. "We're rather crowded on this side of town, Mr. Hedger."

"Well, the parking situation is kind of bad all over. It's no better where I live. I guess we're a nation with too many cars."

Mr. Hedger immediately regretted his words. They had been innocent enough, but he remembered that the Apostle was supposed to own several limousines and station wagons. If the Apostle was offended, however, he gave no indication. "Could be, Mr. Hedger," he said, still grinning amiably.

Abruptly the Apostle clasped his fingers together on the polished desktop as in supplication. It was, it turned out, a misleading gesture. He had a point to press. "You were obviously surprised to find me in a business suit rather than in ceremonial robes, Mr. Hedger . . ."

"Well, I was a little surprised," Mr. Hedger admitted warily.

"The costumes are for my followers, Mr. Hedger. The fancy clothes remind them that their ancestors were once kings, long ago, back in the days of Solomon and Sheba. The Mali Empire. The kingdom of Benin. They like to be reminded of such things . . ."

Mr. Hedger was silent. He did not know where the Apostle's recitation was leading.

"I'm in the public service, Mr. Hedger," the Apostle continued. "The public I serve likes pageantry and frills because it also brings a bit of glamor to their lives. They work hard, and life is not easy for them. I try to help lift their morale and give them a little hope."

Mr. Hedger shifted uneasily. He hoped the Apostle would not feel it necessary to convince him of his piety, but he listened dutifully, studying the black face. He noticed that the small eyes actually were lashless and red as if bloodshot, and that a smudge the color of Miss Shell's lipstick covered one corner of the mouth. The Apostle finished his little speech and reared back in the elevated chair, the grin intact. "I do want to make things clear," he said.

"I understand, sir," Mr. Hedger said, not understanding at all. He decided to get to the point without further delay. "As my secretary indicated, my firm, Keene and Associates, represents the Summit Meat Products Company. They produce a wide assortment of quality meats —sausages, lunch meats, that sort of thing. Perhaps you're familiar with some of them?"

"Yes, I know . . ."

"Well, if you've tried them, it might help my cause if you liked them," Mr. Hedger said brightly. But it was impossible to know if this intended humor amused the Apostle because the face merely held the same grin.

The Apostle shook his shiny head. "I'm sorry, Mr. Hedger, but I never ate any of your products. I've seen them advertised. That's all."

"Well, we're remedying that at once. We're having a special assortment delivered to you this afternoon."

"That is kind of you."

"Well, we certainly hope you'll like them, Apostle Lovett. You see, we're asking you to endorse our products."

The grin contracted for a fleet moment then settled again in its groove. "Why me, Mr. Hedger?"

Mr. Hedger smiled shyly. "Well, frankly, because you're one of the most popular personalities in town, and if you think our products are all right, that'll be good enough recommendation for a whole lot of people."

The Apostle unclasped and reclasped his fingers. He considered a moment. "Perhaps you overestimate my influence, Mr. Hedger. People believe in me because I tell them good things. I tell them things to help them. That doesn't mean they will necessarily do what I do, or even what I want them to do . . ."

"You're being modest, Apostle Lovett. Your followers would do anything you asked them."

The Apostle shook his head again, manipulating his fingers like a fan. "Perhaps. Perhaps. People are kind to me ,as you can see, Mr. Hedger. They have provided me with many of life's material comforts —this nice house here, for example—and it gives me great spiritual comfort to feel I am of some help to them. I'm grateful to them. But they have faith in me only because they know I will not deceive them."

"Well, in endorsing Summit meats you certainly wouldn't be deceiving anybody." Mr. Hedger was aware of the hollow sound of this claim and added quickly: "And we're prepared to make a substantial contribution for your endorsement."

"How substantial?"

The alert response heartened Mr. Hedger. "Well, we have two contracts. The first offers five hundred dollars, the second a thousand . . ."

"Substantial, Mr. Hedger?"

Mr. Hedger stared blankly at the Apostle. He had not imagined the man might consider a thousand dollars inconsequential. He recalled Miss Henderson's warnings with annoyance and directed his irritation at the Apostle's ineradicable grin. "This is a local company," he said. "We've never paid anyone more than a thousand dollars for an endorsement of this kind. We sometimes get endorsements from prominent people for a year's supply of meats, or even less than that . . ."

"I don't think a thousand dollars is a very substantial sum of money, Mr. Hedger."

Mr. Hedger sank back in the lounge chair. "I wish somebody would offer *me* a thousand dollars just for the use of *my* name and picture!"

"I wish that for you also, Mr. Hedger. However, *I* am not *you*."

Mr. Hedger fumbled in his pockets and brought out his cigarettes. It gave him something to do with his hands while mute epithets marched through his head. Then, realizing that the Apostle might object to his smoking, he asked if he could.

"Yes, of course, Mr. Hedger." The Apostle pushed an ashtray toward his guest.

"Would you care for a cigarette, sir?"

"No, thank you."

Mr. Hedger lighted the cigarette and inhaled deeply, averting his eyes from the face across the desk. His glance fell on his briefcase lying unopened at his feet with all the brochures and illustrations of Summit meats inside. There had been no opportunity to display them, and now it was perhaps just as well. He raised his eyes and said: "Then we can't do business?"

The Apostle's grin for once broadened. He even laughed softly. "I didn't say that, Mr. Hedger."

"But you said . . ."

"I said I didn't think a thousand dolars a substantial sum of money. That's what I said." He leaned forward over his clasped hands. "Mr. Hedger, there are dozens of objects inside this house that cost over a thousand dollars."

"But will you consider endorsing our products? We can't offer more."

"I *am* considering it, Mr. Hedger. Money is very useful."

Mr. Hedger sighed, relieved. He decided to press forward. "Well, this is rather urgent, Apostle Lovett. I mean, we're trying to get our posters and ads placed before Memorial Day and the start of the vacation season. Do you think you could let us know in a few days? Say, a week?".

"I can let you know this morning, Mr. Hedger."

"Oh, splendid! That would be splendid!"

Mr. Hedger scooped up his briefcase and extracted the illustrations, spreading them across the desk. "These are actual photographs taken in Summit's test kitchens. Samples of all these meats will be delivered to you this afternoon."

The Apostle rummaged through the slick colored sheets perfunctorily. Then he pushed them aside and reclasped his hands, fixing Mr. Hedger with the inscrutable grin.

"Would you like to go over the contracts?" Mr. Hedger said, excited by the possibility of concluding negotiations at once. He drew the contracts from the briefcase and, selecting the thousand dollar one, proceeded to explain it. "With this contract, Apostle Lovett, we agree to pay you a thousand dollars for your signed endorsement of Summit meats and the right . . ."

"Mr. Hedger . . ."

". . . Yes?"

"Just one question, Mr. Hedger, if you don't mind . . ."

". . . Yes?"

"Does the Summit Meats Products Company employ Negroes?"

Mr. Hedger felt suspended, as if the floor had been whisked from beneath his feet. "Well, I don't know for sure, but they're a very progressive and fair-minded company, and I'm sure they have nothing against employing Negroes . . ."

There was a twinkle in the Apostle's muddy eyes. "Would you find out, Mr. Hedger?"

Mr. Hedger swallowed. "I sure will," he said. "I'll find out as soon as I get back to the office . . ."

The Apostle shook his head. "Now, Mr. Hedger. Would you find out now?' '

Once in the third grade Clyde Hedger had been caught throwing chalk across the classroom. To punish him, the teacher had led him to the officer and made him telephone his mother and tell her what he had done. Now, staring at the telephone, he had the same sensation of helplessness and doom. He picked up the receiver and, when Miss Shell's voice responded, gave her Summit's number. A moment later he had his connection. "Give me Mr. Koscinski, please."

Waiting for Mr. Koscinski's voice, Mr. Hedger forced himself to look at the Apostle. The imperturbable grin suddenly reminded him of the disembodied leer of the Cheshire cat. The malicious thought eased his frustration.

Then Mr. Koscinski spoke and Mr. Hedger braced himself, keeping his voice casual. "Clyde Hedger, Mr. Koscinski . . . I'm at Apostle Lovett's now . . . Could you tell me offhand how many Negroes work at Summit?"

He listened sinkingly as the other voice, hesitant, embarrassed at the question and at the inevitable answer, evaded a direct reply, explaining, "We've often considered hiring some of them, Clyde, but, well, the regular people would object . . . They wouldn't want to work with them . . . And we have to avoid trouble . . ."

"Yes, thank you, Mr. Koscinski."

Mr. Hedger lowered the phone from his ear and slowly—while Mr. Koscinski's voice was still audible, making some further explanation—replaced it in its cradle. He did not look at the Apostle, his eyes might have been closed. He felt defeated—and resentful. The grinning face mocked and accused him, lumped him among the conspirators in a plot for which he shared no responsibility. At last he raised his eyes to meet the Apostle's in a gesture of lost defiance. "They don't hire Negroes," he said.

The Apostle made no immediate response. He sat Buddha-still. But after a moment he unclasped his fingers and, shrugging his narrow shoulders, spread his hands in an expression of regret. "Then we *can't* do business, Mr. Hedger."

Although he knew this would be the answer, a blood-scalding

sensation burned Mr. Hedger's skin. His temples throbbed and his pulse raced. Nevertheless, he calmly swept up his papers and stuffed them in his briefcase. "Well, thank you for your time," he said, standing up.

"It was nothing, Mr. Hedger," the Apostle said. "I wish I could have helped you. As I explained to you, I find money very useful. But I'm a discreet man. I keep faith with my followers."

"Yes, of course."

Mr. Hedger turned to go, wanting to avoid further confrontation with the ugly face, but the Apostle's voice pulled him around again. "Mr. Hedger . . ."

". . . Mr. Hedger, I won't agree to endorse your meats," the voice said. "But then, I will make no mention of the fact that your company has a white-only employment policy. In that way, I will be helping you still."

The two-pronged blade of spite and condescension cut deeply into Mr. Hedger's composure. A flaming, unfamiliar emotion raged inside him. To the black man behind the desk he said a curt, "Good day," and walked away.

"Goodby, Mr. Hedger," the now-hated voice came after him.

Mr. Hedger crossed the shadowed room to the door, opened and closed it behind him without looking back. Miss Shell was sitting cross-legged on the couch. He nodded at her, leaving her low-pitched, "Goodby Mr. Hedger," unacknowledged, letting himself into the hallway. The major-domo in the blue suit jumped to attention, flashing the wide smile as he held open the door. "Good morning, sir." Mr. Hedger nodded, thinking, "That goddam tribal grin!"

As Mr. Hedger walked toward his car, an airplane roared overhead, gaining altitude on its journey to some other city. He watched it glittering in the sun and tried to read the insignia on its side. At the sidewalk, he almost collided with someone and, turning automatically to apologize, saw that it was a little boy.

The boy, no higher than Mr. Hedger's elbow, had the face of an elf and the color of ginger bread. He stood just beyond Mr. Hedger's reach, staring at him with eyes as big and dark as a calf's. Under his arm he cradled a loaf of bread, holding it so tightly that it bulged perilously at each end.

Mr. Hedger's apology died unspoken. He met the boy's unwavering gaze, standing as still as stone. The boy, aping Mr. Hedger, froze motionless too. After a moment, though, he drawled, "Good morning, white man," and walked back slowly, alerted for flight. He stretched his mouth in a mocking grin and began to chant, "Good morning, Mr. White Man, Good Morning, Mr. White Man, Good Morning, Mr. White Man," the tempo rising with his backward speed. Finally, he whirled around and, still singing the ridiculous greeting, sprinted along the sidewalk and across the littered lawn of one of the big houses.

Mr. Hedger watched the boy vanish into the building, and the dark emotion that had been rioting in him discovered its catharsis. "The grinning little nigger!" he said out loud, the words pouring forth deliciously.

Mr. Hedger climbed into his car and drove northward toward the crosstown expressway. He made a mental note to have Miss Henderson cancel the delivery of Summit meats to the Apostle. He wondered what she would say.

John Howard Griffin

is the author of two novels, *The Devil Rides Outside* and *Nuni*. Born in 1920, Mr. Griffin has lived most of his life in Texas. In addition to his most recent work, *Black Like Me*, he has written *Land of the High Sky*.

Dark journey

BY DARK I was away from the beach area and out in the country. Strangely, I began getting rides. Men would pass you in daylight but pick you up after dark.

I must have had a dozen rides that evening. They blear into a nightmare, the one scarcely distinguishable from the other.

It quickly became obvious why they picked me up. All but two picked me up the way they would pick up a pornographic photograph or book—except that this was verbal pornography. With a Negro, they assumed they need give no semblance of self-respect or respectability. The visual element entered into it. In a car at night visibility is reduced. A man will reveal himself in the dark, which gives an illusion of anonymity, more than he will in the bright light. Some were shamelessly open, some shamelessly subtle. All showed morbid curiosity about the sexual life of the Negro, and all had, at base, the same stereotyped image of the Negro as an inexhaustible sex-machine with oversized genitals and a vast store of experiences, immensely varied. They appeared to think that the Negro has done all of those "special" things they themselves have never dared to do. They carried the conversation into the depths of depravity. I note these things because it is harrowing to see decent-looking men and boys assume that because a man is black they need show him none of the reticences they would, out of respect, show the most derelict white man. I note them, too, because they differed completely from the "bull session" men customarily have among themselves. These latter, no matter how frank, have generally a robust tone that says: "We are men, this is an enjoyable thing to do and to discuss, but it will never impugn the basic respect we give one another; it will never distort our humanity." In this, the atmosphere, no matter how coarse, has a verve and an essential joviality that casts out morbidity. It implies respect for the persons involved. But all that I could see here were men shorn of respect either for themselves or their companion.

In my grogginess and exhaustion, these conversations became ghoulish. Each time one of them let me out of his car, I hoped the next would spare me his pantings. I remained mute and pleaded my exhaustion and lack of sleep.

"I'm so tired, I just can't think," I would say.

Like men who had promised themselves pleasure, they would not be denied. It became a strange sort of hounding as they nudged my skull for my sexual reminiscences.

"Well, did you ever do such-and-such?"

"I don't know . . ." I moaned.

"What's the matter—haven't you got any manhood? My old man told me you wasn't really a man till you'd done such-and-such."

Or the older ones, hardened, cynical in their lechery. "Now, don't try to kid me. I wasn't born yesterday. You know you've done such-and-such, just like I have. Hell, it's good that way. Tell me, did you ever get a white woman?"

"Do you think I'm crazy?" I tacitly denied the racist's contention, for he would not hesitate to use it against the Negroes in his conversations around town: "Why, I had one of them admit to me just last night that he craves white women."

"I didn't ask if you was crazy," he said. "I asked if you ever had one—or ever really wanted one." Then, conniving, sweet-toned, "There's plenty white women would like to have a good buck Negro."

"A Negro'd be asking for the rope to get himself mixed up with white women."

"You're just telling me that, but I'll bet inside you think differently . . ."

"This is sure beautiful country through here. What's the main crop?"

"*Don't* you? You can tell me. Hell, I don't care."

"No sir," I sighed.

"You're lying in your teeth and you know it."

Silence. Soon after, almost abruptly he halted the car and said, "Okay, this is as far as I go." He spoke as though he resented my uncooperative attitude, my refusal to give him this strange verbal sexual pleasure.

I thanked him for the ride and stepped down onto the highway. He drove on in the same direction.

Soon another picked me up, a young man in his late twenties who spoke with an educated flair. His questions had the spurious elevation of a scholar seeking information, but the information he sought was entirely sexual, and presupposed that in the ghetto the Negro's life is one of marathon sex with many different partners, open to the view of all; in a word, that marital fidelity and sex as love's goal of union with the beloved object were exclusively the white man's property. Though he pretended to be above such ideas as racial superiority and spoke with genuine warmth, the entire context of his talk reeked of preconceived ideas to the contrary.

"I understand Negroes are much more broad-minded about such things," he said warmly.

"I don't know."

"I understand you make more of an art—or maybe *hobby* out of your sex than we do."

"I doubt it."

"Well, you people don't seem to have the inhibitions we have. We're all basically puritans. I understand Negroes do a lot more things —different kinds of sex—than we do. Oh, don't get me wrong. I admire your attitude, think it's basically healthier than ours. You don't get so damned many *conflicts*. Negroes don't have much neuroses, do they? I mean you people have a more realistic tradition about sex— you're not so sheltered from it as we are."

I knew that what he really meant was that Negroes grew up seeing it from infancy. He had read the same stories, the same reports of social workers about parents sharing a room with children, the father coming home drunk and forcing the mother onto the bed in full view of the young ones. I felt like laughing in his face when I thought of the Negro families I had known already as a Negro: the men on the streets, in the ghettos, the housewives and their great concern that their children "grow up right."

"You people regard sex as a *total* experience—and that's how it should be. Anything that makes you feel good is morally all right for you. Isn't that the main difference?"

"I don't think there's any difference," I said cautiously, not wanting to test the possibility of his wrath at having a Negro disagree with him.

"You *don't?*" His voice betrayed excitement and eagerness; gave no hint of offense.

"Our ministers preach sin and hell just as much as yours," I said. "We've got the same puritanical background as you. We worry just as much as white people about our children losing their virginity or being perverted. We've got the same miserable little worries and problems over our sexual effectiveness, the same guilts that you have."

He appeared astonished and delighted, not at what I said but at the fact that I could say it. His whole attitude of enthusiasm practically shouted, "Why, you talk *intelligently!*" He was so obtuse he did not realize the implied insult in his astonishment that a black man could do anything but say "yes sir" and mumble four-letter words.

Again, he asked questions scarcely different from those that white men would ask themselves; especially scholars who would discuss cultural differences on a detached plane. Yet here the tone was subtly conniving. He went through the motions of courteous research, but he could not hide his real preoccupation. He asked about the size of Negro genitalia and the details of Negro sex life. Only the language differed from the previous inquirers—the substance was the same. The difference was that here I could disagree with him without risking a flood of abuse or petulance. He quoted Kinsey and others. It became apparent he was one of those young men who possess an impressive store of facts, but no truths. This again would have no significance and would be unworthy of note except for one thing: I have talked with such men many times as a white and they never show the glow of prurience he revealed. The significance lay in the fact that my blackness and his concepts of what my blackness implied allowed him to expose himself in this manner. He saw the Negro as a different species. He saw me as something akin to an animal in that he felt no need to maintain his sense of human dignity, though certaintly he would have denied this.

I told myself that I was tired, that I must not judge these men who picked me up and for the price of a ride submitted me to the swamps of their fantasy lives. They showed me something that all men have but seldom bring to the surface, since most men seek health. The boy ended up wanting me to expose myself to him, saying he had never seen a Negro naked. I turned mute, indrawn, giving no answer. The silence rattled between us and I felt sorry for the reprimand that grew from me to him in the silence. I did not want this cruelty to him, since I knew that he showed me a side of his nature that was special to the night and the situation, a side rarely brought to light in his everyday living. I stared at the dimly lighted car dashboard and saw him attending an aunt's funeral, having Sunday dinner with his parents, doing some kindness for a friend—for he was kind. How could I let him see that I understood and that I still respected him, and that I formed no judgment against him for this momentary slip? For instead of seeing it as a manifestation of some poor human charity, he might view it as confirmation that Negroes are insensitive to sexual aberration, that they think nothing of it—

and this would carry on the legend that has so handicapped the Negro.

"I wasn't going to do anything to you," he said in a voice lifeless with humiliation. "I'm not a queer or anything."

"Of course not," I said. "It's nothing."

"It's just that I don't get a chance to talk to educated Negroes—people that can answer questions."

"You make it more complicated than it is," I said. "If you want to know about the sexual morals of the Negro—his practices and ideals —it's no mystery. These are human matters, and the Negro is the same human as the white man. Just ask yourself how it is for a white man and you'll know all the answers. Negro trash is the same as white trash. Negro decency is about the same, too."

"But there are differences. The social studies I've read . . ."

"They don't deal with any basic difference in human nature between black and white," I said. "They only study the effects of environment on human nature. You place the white man in the ghetto, deprive him of educational advantages, arrange it so he has to struggle hard to fulfill his instinct for self-respect, give him little physical privacy and less leisure, and he would after a time assume the same characteristics you attach to the Negro. These characteristics don't spring from whiteness or blackness, but from a man's conditioning."

"Yes, but Negroes have more illegitimate children, earlier loss of virginity and more crime—these are established facts," he insisted without unkindness.

"The fact that the white race has the same problems proves these are not Negro characteristics, but the product of our condition as men," I said. "When you force humans into a subhuman mode of existence, this always happens. Deprive a man of any contact with the pleasures of the spirit and he'll fall completely into those of the flesh."

"But we don't deprive you people of the 'pleasures of the spirit,' " he said.

"In most places we can't go to the concerts, the theater, the museums, public lectures . . . or even to the library. Our schools in the South don't compare to the white schools, poor as they are. You deprive a man of educational opportunities and he'll have no knowledge of the great civilizing influences of art, history, literature and philosophy. Many Negroes don't even know these things exist. With practically nothing to exalt the mind or exercise the spirit, any man is going to sink to his lowest depths. It becomes vicious—and tragic."

"I can't imagine how it must be," he said. "I don't think it's fair. But just the same, plenty of whites don't have access to these things— to art, history, literature and philosophy. Some of the finest people I know live in the country where they never get to museums, concerts."

"Living in the country, they are surrounded by natural museums and concerts," I said. "Besides, those doors are always open to them. The Negro, too, fares better in the country. But most are deprived of education. Ignorance keeps them poor, and when a town-dwelling Negro is poor, he lives in the ghetto. His wife has to work usually, and this leaves the children without parental companionship. In such places, where all of man's time is spent just surviving, he rarely knows what it means to read a great book. He has grown up and now sees his children grow up in squalor. His wife usually earns more than he. He is thwarted in his need to be father-of-the-household. When he looks at his children and his home, he feels the guilt of not having given them something better. His only salvation is not to give a damn finally, or else he will fall into despair. In despair a man's sense of virtue is dulled. He no longer cares. He will do anything to escape it—steal or commit acts of violence—or perhaps try to lose himself in sensuality. Most often the sex-king is just a poor devil trying to prove the manhood that his whole existence denies. This is what the whites call the 'sorry nigger.' Soon he will either desert his home or become so unbearable he is kicked out. This leaves the mother to support the children alone. To keep food in their bellies, she has to spend most of her time away from them, working. This leaves the children to the streets, prey to any sight, any conversation, any sexual experiment that comes along to make their lives more interesting or pleasurable. To a young girl who has nothing, has never known anything, the baubles she can get—both in a kind of crude affection and in gifts or money —by granting sex to a man or boy appeal to her as toys to a child. She gets pregnant sometimes and the vicious circle is given impetus. In some instances the mother cannot make enough to support her children so she sells her sex for what she can get. This gets easier and easier until she comes up with still another child to abort or support. But none of this is 'Negro-ness.'"

"I don't know . . ." he sighed. "It looks like a man could do better."

"It looks that way to you, because you can see what would be better. The Negro knows something is terribly wrong, but with things the way they are, he can't know that something better actually exists on the other side of work and study. We are all born blank. It's the same for blacks or whites or any other shade of man. Your blanks have been filled in far differently from those of a child grown up in the filth and poverty of the ghetto."

He drove without speaking through a thundershower that crinkled the windshield and raised the hum of his tires an octave.

"But the situation is changing," I said after a time. "The Negro may not understand exactly *how*, but he knows one thing—the only way out of this tragedy is through education, training. Thousands of them sacrifice everything to get the education, to prove once and for all that the Negro's capacity for learning, for accomplishment, is equal to that of any other man—that the pigment has nothing to do with degrees of intelligence, talent or virtue. This isn't just wishful thinking. It's been proved conclusively in every field."

"We don't hear about those things," he said.

"I know. Southern newspapers print every rape, attempted rape, suspected rape and 'maybe rape,' but outstanding accomplishment is not considered newsworthy. Even the Southern Negro has little chance to know this, since he reads the same slanted reports in the news-papers."

The young man slowed to a halt in a little settlement to let me out.

"I'm sorry about a while ago—I don't know what got into me," he said.

"I've already forgotten it."

"No offense?"

"No offense."

"Okay. Good luck to you."

I thanked him and stepped out onto the wet neon reflections of the road. The air, cool and mist-filled, surrounded me with its freshness. I watched the red tail-light of his car fog into the distance.

I had no time to worry about sitting down or getting a sandwich. An old-model car tooted its horn and skidded to a stop a few yards beyond me. The smell of a rainy Alabama night, the succession of sexual oddments turned me suddenly sick with dread at what this stranger would want. But I had no alternative. There was no place there to sleep.

"Where you going?" he asked.

"Mobile," I said. He told me to get in. I glanced through the glassless window to see a heavy-set, round-faced, tough-looking young man.

As we drove, the tensions drained from me. He was boisterous, loud and guileless. I could only conclude that he was color blind, since he appeared unaware that I was a Negro. He enjoyed company, nothing more. He told me he was a construction worker and tonight he was late getting home to his wife and infant son. "I couldn't get this sonofabitching rattletrap to go," he said. "I leave the good car at home for my wife."

For an hour we delighted ourselves with talk of our children. The experience of parenthood filled him with enthusiasm and he recited the endless merits of his son and drew me out to tell him of my children.

"I can see I'm not going to make it without something to eat," he said. "I'm usually home by six and my wife has supper on the table. You had any supper?"

"No, I sure haven't."

"You want a hamburger?"

"I don't think there's any place here that would serve me."

"Shit, I'll bring it to the car. We can eat while I'm driving."

I watched him walk into a roadside café. He looked young, not over twenty, and I wondered how he had escaped the habit of guarded fencing that goes on constantly between whites and Negroes in the South wherever they meet. He was the first man I met of either color who did not confuse the popular image of the thing with the thing itself.

I wondered where he got this, and sought to discover the source of his attitude during the drive into Mobile. His background, his education and his home were ordinary. On the car radio he played with relish the twang-twang blues type of music and his TV preferences were westerns. "Oh, hell, I can't go for those old heavy dramas." Perhaps his religion? "My wife's a Presbyterian. Sometimes I go with her. But I don't much like it." Perhaps his reading?

"Have you got a good library in Mobile?"

"I don't know, to tell you the truth. I think it's supposed to be pretty good. My wife reads a lot."

I could only conclude that his attitude came from an overwhelming love for his child, so profound it spilled over to all humanity. I knew that he was totally unaware of its ability to cure men; of the blessings it could be to someone like me after having been exhausted and scraped raw in my heart by others this rainy Alabama night.

I thought of Maritain's conclusion that the only solution to the problems of man is the return of charity (in the old embracing sense of *caritas*, not in the stingy literal sense it has assumed in our language and in our days) and metaphysics. Or, more simply, the maxim of St. Augustine: "Love, and then do what you will."

To live in a world where men do not love, where they cheat and are callous, is to sink into a preoccupation with death, and to see the futility of anything except virtue. When I crossed the line from Mississippi into Alabama, I felt as though I were leaving a cemetery.

Chester Himes

now living in Paris, published his first novel, *If He Hollers Let Him Go*, in 1945. Thirteen other novels at least, have followed along with many articles, many of them for the French press. He has also been associated with the French film industry. A close friend and confidante of the late Richard Wright, Himes was one of the pillars of the famous Olympia Press. His latest novel was *The Heat's On*.

Dilemma of the negro novelist in U.S.

ANY DISCUSSION of the Negro novelists in the U.S.A. must first examine the reasons why all novelists, whatever their race and nationality, write. The obvious answer, the one that first comes to mind, is that we write to express and perpetuate our intellectual and emotional experiences, our observations and conclusions. We write to relate to others the process of our thoughts, the creations of our imaginings. That is the pat answer.

We have a greater motive, a nobler aim; we are impelled by a higher cause. We write not only to express our experiences, our intellectual processes, but to interpret the meaning contained in them. We search for the meaning of life in the realities of our experiences, in the realities of our dreams, our hopes, our memories. Beauty finds reality in the emotion it produces, but that emotion must be articulated before we can understand it. Anger and hatred require expression as do love and charity.

The essential necessity of humanity is to find justification for existence. Man cannot live without some knowledge of the purpose of life. If he can find no purpose in life he creates one in the inevitability of death. We are maintained at our level of nobility by our incessant search for ourselves.

The writer seeks an interpretation of the whole of life from the sum of his experiences. When his experiences have been so brutalized, restricted, degraded, when his very soul has been so pulverized by oppression, his summations can not avoid bitterness, fear, hatred, protest; he is inclined to reveal only dwarfed, beaten personalities and life that is bereft of all meaning. But his logic will tell him that humanity can not accept the fact of existence without meaning. He must find the meaning regardless of the quality of his experiences. Then begins his slow, tortured progress toward truth.

The Negro writer, more than any other, is faced with this necessity. He must discover from his experiences the truth of his oppressed existence in terms that will provide some meaning to his life. Why he is here; why he continues to live. In fact, this writer's subject matter is in reality a Negro's search for truth.

From the start the American Negro writer is beset by conflicts. He is in conflict with himself, with his environment, with his public. The personal conflict will be the hardest. He must decide at the outset the extent of his honesty. He will find it no easy thing to reveal the truth of his experience or even to discover it. He will derive no pleasure from the recounting of his hurts. He will encounter more agony by his explorations into his own personality than most non-Negroes realize. For him to delineate the degrading effects of oppression will be like inflicting a wound upon himself. He will have begun an intellectual crusade that will take him through the horrors of the damned. And this must be his reward for his integrity: he will be reviled by the Negroes and whites alike. Most of all, he will find no valid interpretation of his experiences in terms of human values until the truth be known.

If he does not discover this truth, his life will be forever veiled in mystery, not only to whites but to himself; and he will be heir to all the weird interpretations of his personality.

The urge to submit to the pattern prescribed by oppression will be powerful. The appeal to retrench, equivocate, compromise, will be issued by friend and foe alike. The temptations to accede will be tempting, the rewards coercive. The oppressor pays, and sometimes well, for the submission of the oppressed.

To the American Negro writer's mind will come readily a number of rationalizations. He may say to himself: "I must free myself of all race consciousness before I can understand the true nature of human experiences, for it is not the Negro problem at all, but the human problem." Or he may attempt to return to African culture, not as a source but as an escape, and say: "This is my culture; I have no other culture." But he will find that he can not accomplish this departure because he is an American. He will realize in the end that he possesses this heritage of slavery; he is a product of this American culture; his thoughts and emotions and reactions have been fashioned by his American environment. He will discover that he can not free himself of race consciousness because he can not free himself of race; that is his motive in attempting to run away. But, to paraphrase a statement of Joe Louis', "He may run, but he can't hide."

Once the writer's inner conflict has been resolved and he has elected the course of honesty, he will begin his search for truth. But the conflict will not cease. He immediately enters into conflict with his environment. Various factors of American life and American culture will be raised to stay his pen. The most immediate of these various conflicts is with the publisher. From a strictly commercial point of view, most publishers consider honest novels by Negro writers on Negro subjects bad ventures. If there is nothing to alleviate the bitter truth, no glossing over of the harsh facts, compromising on the vital issues, most publishers feel that the book will not sell. And the average publisher today will not publish a novel he thinks will not sell.

However, should the Negro find a publisher guided by neither profit nor prejudice (a very rare publisher indeed), he may run into the barrier of preconception. Many truly liberal white people are strongly opinionated on the racial theme, and consider as false or overdrawn any conception that does not agree with their own. Ofttimes these people feel that their experiences *with* Negroes (unfortunately not *as* Negroes) establish them as authorities on the subject. But quite often their opinions are derived from other Negroes who have attained financial success or material security, in fact fame and great esteem, through a trenchant sort of dishonesty, an elaborate and highly convincing technique of modern uncle-tomism. It is unfortunate that so many white people who take an active and sympathetic interest in the solution of the American racial dilemma become indoctrinated first by such Negroes. Instead of receiving a true picture of Negroes' personalities, they are presented with comforting illusions. Should the publisher be of this group, he concludes that the honest Negro writer is psychotic, that his evaluations are based on personal experiences which are in no way typical of his race. This publisher does not realize that his own reasoning is self-contradictory; that any American Negro's racial experience, be they psychotic or not, are typical of all Negroes' racial experiences for the simple reason that the source is not the Negro but oppression.

Then there is, of course, the publisher with such a high content of racial bias as to reject violently any work that does not present the Negro as a happy contented soul. But there will be no conflict between the Negro writer and this publisher; it will never begin.

Once the writer's work is past the printer, his inner conflict having been resolved and his publisher convinced, there begins a whole turbulent sea of conflict between the novelist and his public.

If this novelist, because he has prepared an honest and revealing work on Negro life anticipates the support and encouragement of middle-class Negro people, he is doomed to disappointment. He must be prepared for the hatred and antagonism of many of his own people, for attacks from his leaders, the clergy and the press; he must be ready to have his name reviled at every level, intellectual or otherwise. This is not hard to understand. The American Negro seeks to hide his beaten, battered soul, his dwarfed personality, his scars of oppression. He does not want it known that he has been so badly injured for fear he will be taken out of the game. The American Negro's highest ambition is to be included in the stream of American life, to be permitted to "play the game" as any other American, and he is opposed to anything he thinks will aid in his exclusion. The American Negro, we must remember, is an American; the face may be the face of Africa, but the heart has the beat of Wall Street.

But Negroes will themselves oppress other Negroes, given the opportunity, in as vile a manner as anyone else. The Negro writer must be able to foresee this reaction. The antagonism and opposition of the white American, he has already expected. These oppressors who have brutally ravaged the personality of a race, dare their victims to reveal the scars thus inflicted. The scars of those assaulted personalities are not only reminders, but affronts.

It is in this guilt which now we all know of and understand, that keeps the oppressor outraged and unrelenting. It is his fear that he will have to resolve a condition which is as much his heritage as slavery is our own. The guilt, revolving in this fear is a condition the oppressor dare not aggravate. Yet, he can not permit or accept it, a fact which traps the white oppressor in his own greatest contradiction. The oppressor can not look upon the effects of his oppression without being aware of this contradiction; he doesn't want to be confronted with this evil, but neither can he escape or resolve it. He will go to any extent, from the bestial to the ridiculous, to avoid confrontation with this issue.

As Horace Cayton wrote in, *Race Conflict in Modern Society.*

"To relieve himself of his guilt, to justify his hate, and to expel his fear, white men have erected an elaborate facade of justifications and rationalizations. The Negro is a primitive, dangerous person who must be kept in subordination. Negroes do not have the same high sensibilities as do whites and do not mind exploitation and rejection. Negroes are passive children of nature and are incapable of participating in and enjoying the higher aspects of the general American culture. Negroes would rather be by themselves. Negroes are eaten with tuberculosis and syphilis. But all these rationalizations do not quell the gnawing knowledge that they, Americans who believe in freedom, believe in the dignity of the human personality, are actively or passively perpetuating a society which defiles all that is human in other human beings."

We already know that attacks upon the honest American Negro novelist will emanate from the white race. However, the tragedy is that among white liberal groups are people who, themselves, are guiltless of any desire to oppress, but suffer the same guilt as do the active oppressors. Because of this they abhor with equal intensity the true revelations of Negroes' personalities. There are, of course, truly thoughtful, sincere, sympathetic white people who will shudder in protest at the statement that all American Negroes hate all American whites.

Of course, Negroes hate white people, far more actively than white people hate Negroes. What sort of idiocy is it that reasons American Negroes don't hate American whites? Can you abuse, enslave, persecute, segregate and generally oppress a people, and have them love you for it? Are white people expected not to hate *their* oppressors? Could any people be expected to escape the natural reaction to oppression? Let us be sensible. To hate white people is one of the first emotions an American Negro develops when he becomes old enough to learn what his status is in American society. He must, of necessity, hate white people. He would not be—and it would not be human if he did not— develop a hatred for his oppressors. At some time in the lives of every American Negro there has been this hatred for white people; there are no exceptions. It could not possibly be otherwise.

To the Negro writer who would plumb the depth of the Negro personality, there is no question of whether Negroes hate white people —but how does this hatred affect the Negro's personality? How much of himself is destroyed by this necessity to hate those who oppress him? Certainly hate is a destructive emotion. In the case of the Negro, hate is doubly destructive. The American Negro experiences two forms of hate. He hates first his oppressor, and then because he lives in constant fear of this hatred being discovered, he hates himself— because of this fear.

Yes, hate is an ugly word. It is an ugly emotion. It would be wonderful to say there is no hate; to say, we do not hate. But to merely speak the words would not make it so; it would not help us, who are Negroes, rid ourselves of hate. It would not help you, who are not Negroes, rid yourselves of hate. And it would not aid in the removal of the causes for which we hate. The question the Negro writer must answer is: how does the fear he feels as a Negro in white American society affect his, the Negro personality?

There can be no understanding of Negro life, of Negroes' compulsions, reactions and actions; there can be no understanding of the sexual impulses, of Negro crime, of Negro marital relations, of our spiritual entreaties, our ambitions and our defeats, until this fear has been revealed at work behind the false fronted facades of our ghettoes; until others have experienced with us to the same extent the impact of fear upon our personalities. It is no longer enough to say the Negro is a victim of a stupid myth. We must know the truth and what it does to us.

If this plumbing for the truth reveals within the Negro personality, homicidal mania, lust for white women, a pathetic sense of inferiority, paradoxical anti-Semitism, arrogance, uncle tomism, hate and fear and self-hate, this then is the effect of oppression on the human personality. These are the daily horrors, the daily realities, the daily experiences of an oppressed minority.

And if it appears that the honest American Negro writer is trying to convince his audience that the whole Negro race in America, as a result of centuries of oppression, is sick at soul, the conclusion is unavoidable. It could not conceivably be otherwise.

The dilemma of the Negro writer lies not so much in what he must reveal, but in the reactions of his audience, in the intellectual limitations of the reader which so often confine men to habit and withhold from them the nobler instruments of reason and conscience. There should be no indictment of the writer who reveals this truth, but of the conditions that have produced it.

Himes logic has noted that American Negroes *have* written honest books and that they have been published and read. That is evidence that the dominant white group in America is not entirely given over to an irrevocable course of oppression.

There is an indomitable quality within the human spirit that can not be destroyed; a face deep within the human personality that is impregnable to all assaults. This quality, this force, exists deep within the Negro also; he is human. They rest so deeply that prejudice, oppression, lynchings, riots, time or weariness can never corrode or destroy them. During the three hundred years Negroes have lived in America as slaves and near subhumans, the whole moral fibre and personality of those Negroes now living would be a total waste; we would be drooling idiots, dangerous maniacs, raving beasts—if it were not for that quality and force within all humans that cries: "I will live!"

There is no other explanation of how so many Negroes have been able to break through the restrictions of oppression, retain their integrity, and attain eminence, and make valuable contributions to our whole culture. The Negro writer must not only reveal the truth, but also reveal and underline these higher qualities of humanity.

My definition of this quality within the human spirit that can not be destroyed is a single word: *Growth.* Growth is the surviving influence in all lives. The tree will send up its trunk in thick profusion from land burned black by atom bombs. Children will grow from poverty and filth and oppression and develop honor, develop integrity, contribute to all mankind.

It is a long way, a hard way from the hatred of the faces to the hatred of evil, a longer way still to the brotherhood of men. Once on the road, however, the Negro will discover that he is not alone. The white people whom he will encounter along the way may not appear to be accompanying him. But all, black and white, will be growing. When the American Negro writer has discovered that nothing ever becomes permanent but change, he will have rounded out his knowledge of the truth. And he will have performed his service as an artist.

Langston Hughes

born in 1902 in Joplin, Missouri is a poet, anthologist and creator of the Simple books—*Simple Speaks His Mind, Simple Takes a Wife* and *Simple Stakes a Claim*. Perhaps the most distinguished member of the "Harlem Renaissance," Mr. Hughes' works have been appearing since 1926.

Name in print

"JUST LOOK at the front pages of the newspapers," said Simple, spreading his nightly copy of the *Daily News* out on the bar. "There is never hardly any colored names anywhere. Most headlines is all about white folks."

"That is not true today," I said. "Many headlines are about Negroes, Chinese, Indians, and other colored folks like ourselves."

"Most on the inside pages," said Simple, blowing foam from his beer. "But I am talking about front-page news. The only time colored folks is front-page news is when there's been a race riot or a lynching or a boycott and a whole lot of us have been butchered up or arrested. Then they announce it."

"You," I said, "have a race phobia. You see prejudice where there is none, and Jim Crow where it doesn't exist. How can you be constructive front-page news if you don't *make* front-page news?"

"How can I make front-page news in a white paper if I am not white?" asked Simple. "Or else I have to be Ralph Bunche or Eartha Kitt. That is why I am glad we have got colored papers like the *Afro, Defender, Courier,* and *Sepia,* so I can be news, too."

"I presume that when you say 'I' you mean the racial I—Negroes. You are not talking about yourself."

"Of course I am not talking about myself," said Simple, draining his glass. "I have never been nowhere near news except when I was in the Harlem Riots. Then the papers did not mention me by name. They just said 'mob.' I were a part of the mob. When the Mayor's Committee report come out, they said I were 'frustrated.' Which is true, I were. It is very hard for a Negro like me to get his name in the news, the reason being that white folks do not let us nowhere near news in the first place. For example, take all these graft investigations that's been going on in Brooklyn and New York every other week, unions and docks, cops and bookies, and million-dollar handouts. Do you read about any Negroes being mixed up in them, getting even a hundred dollars of them millions, or being called up before the grand jury? You do not. White folks are just rolling in graft! But where are the Negroes? Nowhere near the news. Irish names, Italian names,

Jewish names, all kinds of names in the headlines every time Judge Liebowitz opens his mouth. Do you read any colored names? The grand jury don't even bother to investigate Harlem. There has never been a million dollars' worth of graft in Harlem in all the years since the Indians sold Manhattan for a handful of beads. Indians and Negroes don't get nowhere near graft, neither into much news. Find me some Negro news in tonight's *News*."

"I would hardly wish to get into the papers if I had to make news by way of graft," I said. "There is nothing about graft of which any race can be proud."

"Our race could do right well with some of that big money, though," said Simple, signaling the barman for another beer. "But it does not have to be graft, in unions or out. I am just using that as an example. Take anything else on the front pages. Take flying saucers in the sky. Everybody but a Negro has seen one. If a Negro did see a flying saucer, I bet the papers wouldn't report it. They probably don't even let flying saucers fly over Harlem, just to keep Negroes from seeing them. This morning in the subway I read where Carl Krubelewski had seen a flying saucer, also Ralph Curio saw one. And way up in Massachusetts a while back, Henry Armpriester seen one. Have you ever read about Roosevelt Johnson or Ralph Butler or Carl Jenkins or anybody that sounded like a Negro seeing one? I did not. Has a flying saucer ever passed over Lenox Avenue? Nary one! Not even Daddy Grace has glimpsed one, neither Mother Horne nor Adam Powell. Negroes can't get on the front page no kind of way. We can't even see a flying saucer."

"It would probably scare the wits out of you, if you did see one," I said, "so you might not live to read your name in the papers."

"I could read my name from the other world then," said Simple, "and be just as proud. Me, Jesse B. Semple—my name in print for once—killed by looking at a flying saucer."

Shirley Jackson

who died in 1964 authored *We Have Always Lived in a Castle* and her most famous work, the chilling *The Lottery*. She was married to critic Edgar Stanley Hyman and they lived in Vermont where many of her stories were set.

Flower garden

AFTER LIVING in an old Vermont manor house together for almost eleven years, the two Mrs. Winnings, mother and daughter-in-law, had grown to look a good deal alike, as women will who live intimately together, and work in the same kitchen and get things done around the house in the same manner. Although young Mrs. Winning had been a Talbot, and had dark hair which she wore cut short, she was now officially a Winning, a member of the oldest family in town and her hair was beginning to grey where her mother-in-law's hair had greyed first, at the temples; they both had thin sharp-featured faces and eloquent hands, and sometimes when they were washing dishes or shelling peas or polishing silverware together, their hands, moving so quickly and similarly, communicated more easily and sympathetically than their minds ever could. Young Mrs. Winning thought sometimes, when she sat at the breakfast table next to her mother-in-law, with her baby girl in the high-chair close by, that they must resemble some stylized block print for a New England wallpaper; mother, daughter, and grand-daughter, with perhaps Plymouth Rock or Concord Bridge in the background.

On this, as on other cold mornings, they lingered over their coffee, unwilling to leave the big kitchen with the coal stove and the pleasant atmosphere of food and cleanliness, and they sat together silently sometimes until the baby had long finished her breakfast and was playing quietly in the special baby corner, where uncounted Winning children had played with almost identical toys from the same heavy wooden box.

"It seems as though spring would never come," young Mrs. Winning said. "I get so tired of the cold."

"Got to be cold some of the time," her mother-in-law said. She began to move suddenly and quickly, stacking plates, indicating that the time for sitting was over and the time for working had begun. Young Mrs. Winning, rising immediately to help, thought for the thousandth time that her mother-in-law would never relinquish the position of authority in her own house until she was too old to move before anyone else.

"And I wish someone would move into the old cottage," young Mrs. Winning added. She stopped halfway to the pantry with the table napkins and said longingly, "If only *someone* would move in before spring." Young Mrs. Winning had wanted, long ago, to buy the cottage herself, for her husband to make with his own hands into a home where they could live with their children, but now, accustomed as she was to the big old house at the top of the hill where her husband's family had lived for generations, she had only a great kindness left toward the little cottage, and a wistful anxiety to see some happy young people living there. When she heard it was sold, as all the old houses were being sold in these days when no one could seem to find a newer place to live, she had allowed herself to watch daily for a sign that someone new was coming; every morning she glanced down from the back porch to see if there was smoke coming out of the cottage chimney, and every day going down the hill on her way to the store she hesitated past the cottage, watching carefully for the least movement within. The cottage had been sold in January and now, nearly two months later, even though it seemed prettier and less worn with the snow gently covering the overgrown garden and icicles in front of the blank windows, it was still forlorn and empty, despised since the day long ago when Mrs. Winning had given up all hope of ever living there.

Mrs. Winning deposited the napkins in the pantry and turned to tear the leaf off the kitchen calendar before selecting a dish towel and joining her mother-in-law at the sink. "March already," she said despondently.

"They *did* tell me down at the store yesterday," her mother-in-law said, "that they were going to start painting the cottage this week."

"Then that *must* mean someone's coming!"

"Can't take more than a couple of weeks to paint inside that little house," old Mrs. Winning said.

It was almost April, however, before the new people moved in. The snow had almost melted and was running down the street in icy, half-solid rivers. The ground was slushy and miserable to walk on, the skies grey and dull. In another month the first amazing green would start in the trees and on the ground, but for the better part of April there would be cold rain and perhaps more snow. The cottage had been painted inside, and new paper put on the walls. The front steps had been repaired and new glass put into the broken windows. In spite of the grey sky and the patches of dirty snow the cottage looked neater and firmer, and the painters were coming back to do the outside when the weather cleared. Mrs. Winning, standing at the foot of the cottage walk, tried to picture the cottage as it stood now, against the picture of the cottage she had many years ago, when she had hoped to live there herself. She had wanted roses by the porch; that could be done, and the neat colorful garden she had planned. She would have painted the outside white, and that too might still be done. Since the cottage had been sold she had not gone inside, but she remembered the little rooms, with the windows over the garden that could be so bright with gay curtains and window boxes, the small kitchen she would have painted yellow, the two bedrooms upstairs with slanting ceilings under the eaves. Mrs. Winning looked at the cottage for a long time, standing on the wet walk, and then went slowly on down to the store.

The first news she had of the new people came, at last, from the grocer a few days later. As he was tieing the string around the three pounds of hamburger the large Winning family would consume in one meal, he asked cheerfully, "Seen your new neighbors yet?"

"Have they moved in?" Mrs. Winning asked. "The people in the cottage?"

"Lady in here this morning," the grocer said. "Lady and a little boy, seem like nice people. They say her husband's dead. Nice-looking lady."

Mrs. Winning had been born in the town and the grocer's father had given her jawbreakers and licorice in the grocery store while the present grocer was still in high school. For a while, when she was twelve and the grocer's son was twenty, Mrs. Winning had hoped secretly that he would want to marry her. He was fleshy now, and middle-aged, and although he still called her Helen and she still called him Tom, she belonged now to the Winning family and had to speak critically to him, no matter how unwillingly, if the meat were tough or the butter price too high. She knew that when he spoke of the new neighbor as a "lady" he meant something different than if he had spoken of her as a "woman" or a "person." Mrs. Winning knew that he spoke of the two Mrs. Winnings to his other customers as "ladies." She hesitated and asked, "Have they really moved in to stay?"

"She'll have to stay for a while," the grocer said drily. "Bought a week's worth of groceries."

Going back up the hill with her package Mrs. Winning watched all the way to detect some sign of the new people in the cottage. When she reached the cottage walk she slowed down and tried to watch not too obviously. There was no smoke coming from the chimney, and no sign of furniture near the house, as there might have been if people were still moving in, but there was a middle-aged car parked in the street before the cottage and Mrs. Winning thought she could see figures moving past the windows. On a sudden irresistible impulse she turned and went up the walk to the front porch, and then, after debating for a moment, on up the steps to the door. She knocked, holding her bag of groceries in one arm, and then the door opened and she looked down on a little boy, about the same age, she thought happily, as her own son.

"Hello," Mrs. Winning said.

"Hello," the boy said. He regarded her soberly.

"Is your mother here?" Mrs. Winning asked. "I came to see if I could help her move in."

"We're all moved in," the boy said. He was about to close the door, but a woman's voice said from somewhere in the house, "Davey? Are you talking to someone?"

"That's my mommy," the little boy said. The woman came up behind him and opened the door a little wider. "Yes?" she said.

Mrs. Winning said, "I'm Helen Winning. I live about three houses up the street, and I thought perhaps I might be able to help you."

"Thank you," the woman said doubtfully. She's younger than I am, Mrs. Winning thought, she's about thirty. And pretty. For a clear minute Mrs. Winning saw why the grocer had called her a lady.

"It's so nice to have someone living in this house," Mrs. Winning said shyly. Past the other woman's head she coud see the small hallway, with the larger living-room beyond and the door on the left going into the kitchen, the stairs on the right, with the delicate stair-rail newly painted; they had done the hall in light green, and Mrs. Winning smiled with friendship at the woman in the doorway, thinking, She *has* done it right; this is the way it should look after all, she knows about pretty houses.

After a minute the other woman smiled back, and said, "Will you come in?"

As she stepped back to let Mrs. Winning in, Mrs. Winning wondered with a suddenly stricken conscience if perhaps she had not been too forward, almost pushing herself in. . . . "I hope I'm not making a nuisance of myself," she said unexpectedly, turning to the other woman. "It's just that I've been wanting to live here myself for so long." Why did I say that, she wondered; it had been a very long time since young Mrs. Winning had said the first thing that came into her head.

"Come see *my* room," the little boy said urgently, and Mrs. Winning smiled down at him.

"I have a little boy just about your age," she said. "What's your name?"

"Davey," the little boy said, moving closer to his mother. "Davey William MacLane."

"My little boy," Mrs. Winning said soberly, "is named Howard Talbot Winning."

The little boy looked up at his mother uncertainly, and Mrs. Winning, who felt ill at ease and awkward in this little house she so longed for, said, "How old are you? My little boy is five."

"I'm five," the little boy said, as though realizing it for the first time. He looked again at his mother and she said graciously, "Will you come in and see what we've done to the house?"

Mrs. Winning put her bag of groceries down on the slim-legged table in the green hall, and followed Mrs. MacLane into the living-room, which was L-shaped and had the windows Mrs. Winning would have fitted with gay curtains and flower-boxes. As she stepped into the room Mrs. Winning realized, with a quick wonderful relief, that it was really going to be all right, after all. Everything, from the andirons in the fireplace to the books on the table, was exactly as Mrs. Winning might have done if she were eleven years younger; a little more informal, perhaps, nothing of quite such good quality as young Mrs. Winning might have chosen, but still richly, undeniably right. There was a picture of Davey on the mantel, flanked by a picture which Mrs. Winning supposed was Davey's father; there was a glorious blue bowl on the low coffe table, and around the corner of the L stood a row of orange plates on a shelf, and a polished maple table and chairs.

"It's lovely," Mrs. Winning said. This could have been mine, she was thinking, and she stood in the doorway and said again, "It's perfectly lovely."

Mrs. MacLane crossed over to the low armchair by the fireplace and picked up the soft blue material that lay across the arm. "I'm making curtains," she said, and touched the blue bowl with the tip of one finger. "Somehow I always make my blue bowl the center of the room," she said. "I'm having the curtains the same blue, and my rug—when it comes!—will have the same blue in the design."

"It matches Davey's eyes," Mrs. Winning said, and when Mrs. MacLane smiled again she saw that it matched Mrs. MacLane's eyes too. Helpless before so much that was magic to her, Mrs. Winning said, "*Have* you painted the kitchen yellow?"

"Yes," Mrs. MacLane said, surprised. "Come and see." She led the way through the L, around past the orange plates to the kitchen, which caught the late morning sun and shone with clean paint and bright aluminum; Mrs. Winning noticed the electric coffepot, the waffle iron, the toaster, and thought, *she* couldn't have much trouble cooking, not with just two of them.

"When I have a garden," Mrs. MacLane said, "we'll be able to see it from almost all the windows." She gestured to the broad kitchen windows, and added, "I love gardens. I imagine I'll spend most of my time working in this one, as soon as the weather is nice."

"It's a good house for a garden," Mrs. Winning said. "I've heard that it used to be one of the prettiest gardens on the block."

"I thought so too," Mrs. MacLane said. "I'm going to have flowers on all four sides of the house. With a cottage like this you can, you know."

Oh, I know, I know, Mrs. Winning thought wistfully, remembering the neat charming garden she could have had, instead of the row of nasturtiums along the side of the Winning house, which she tended so carefully; no flowers would grow well around the Winning house, because of the heavy old maple trees which shaded all the yard and which had been tall when the house was built.

Mrs. MacLane had had the bathroom upstairs done in yellow, too, and the two small bedrooms with overhanging eaves were painted green and rose. "All garden colors," she told Mrs. Winning gaily, and Mrs. Winning, thinking of the oddly-matched, austere bedrooms in the big Winning house, sighed and admitted that it would be wonderful to have window seats under the eaves windows. Davey's bedroom was the green one, and his small bed was close to the window. "This morning," he told Mrs. Winning solemnly, "I looked out and there were four icicles hanging by my bed."

Mrs. Winning stayed in the cottage longer than she should have; she felt certain, although Mrs. MacLane was pleasant and cordial, that her visit was extended past courtesy and into curiosity. Even so, it was only her sudden guilt about the three pounds of hamburger and dinner for the Winning men that drove her away. When she left, waving good-bye to Mrs. MacLane and Davey as they stood in the cottage doorway, she had invited Davey up to play with Howard, Mrs. MacLane up for tea, both of them to come for lunch some day, and all without the permission of her mother-in-law.

Reluctantly she came to the big house and turned past the bolted front door to go up the walk to the back door which all the family used in the winter. Her mother-in-law looked up as she came into the kitchen and said irritably, "I called the store and Tom said you left an hour ago."

"I stopped off at the old cottage," Mrs. Winning said. She put the package of groceries down on the table and began to take things out quickly, to get the doughnuts on to a plate and the hamburger into the pan before too much time was lost. With her coat still on and her scarf over her head she moved as fast as she could while her mother-in-law, slicing bread at the kitchen table, watched her silently.

"Take your coat off," her mother-in-law said finally. "Your husband will be home in a minute."

By twelve o'clock the house was noisy and full of mud tracked across the kitchen floor. The oldest Howard, Mrs. Winning's father-in-law, came in from the farm and went silently to hang his hat and coat in the dark hall before speaking to his wife and daughter-in-law; the younger Howard, Mrs. Winning's husband, came in from the barn after putting the truck away and nodded to his wife and kissed his mother; and the youngest Howard, Mrs. Winning's son, crashed into the kitchen, home from kindergarten, shouting, "Where's dinner?"

The baby, anticipating food, banged on her high-chair with the silver cup which had first been used by the oldest Howard Winning's mother. Mrs. Winning and her mother-in-law put plates down on the table swiftly, knowing after many years the exact pause between the latest arrival and the serving of food, and with a minimum of time three generations of the Winning family were eating silently and efficiently, all anxious to be back about their work: the farm, the mill, the electric train; the dishes, the sewing, the nap. Mrs. Winning, feeding the baby, trying to anticipate her mother-in-law's gestures of serving, thought, today more poignantly than ever before, that she had at least given them another Howard, with the Winning eyes and mouth, in exchange for her food and her bed.

After dinner, after the men had gone back to work and the

children were in bed, the baby for her nap and Howard resting with crayons and coloring book, Mrs. Winning sat down with her mother-in-law over their sewing and tried to describe the cottage.

"It's just perfect," she said helplessly: "Everything is so pretty. She invited us to come down some day and see it when it's all finished, the curtains and everything."

"I was talking to Mrs. Blake," the elder Mrs. Winning said, as though in agreement. "She says the husband was killed in an automobile accident. *She* had some money in her own name and I guess she decided to settle down in the country for the boy's health. Mrs. Blake said he looked peakish."

"She loves gardens," Mrs. Winning said, her needle still in her hand for a moment. "She's going to have a big garden all around the house."

"She'll need help," the elder woman said humorlessly, "that's a mightly big garden she'll have."

"She has the *most* beautiful blue bowl, Mother Winning. You'd love it, it's almost like silver."

"Probably," the elder Mrs. Winning said after a pause, "probably her people came from around here a ways back, and *that's* why she's settled in these parts."

The next day Mrs. Winning walked slowly past the cottage, and slowly the next, and the day after, and the day after that. On the second day she saw Mrs. MacLane at the window, and waved, and on the third day she met Davey on the sidewalk. "When are you coming to visit my little boy?" she asked him, and he stared at her solemnly and said, "Tomorrow."

Mrs. Burton, next-door to the MacLanes, ran over on the third day they were there with a fresh apple pie, and then told all the neighbors about the yellow kitchen and the bright electric utensils. Another neighbor, whose husband had helped Mrs. MacLane start her furnace, explained that Mrs. MacLane was only very recently widowed. One or another of the townspeople called on the MacLanes almost daily, and frequently, as young Mrs. Winning passed, she saw familiar faces at the windows, measuring the blue curtains with Mrs. MacLane, or she waved to acquaintances who stood chatting with Mrs. MacLane on the now firm front steps. After the MacLanes had been in the cottage for about a week Mrs. Winning met them one day in the grocery and they walked up the hill together, and talked about putting Davey into the kindergarten. Mrs. MacLane wanted to keep him home as long as possible, and Mrs. Winning asked her, "Don't you feel terribly tied down, having him with you all the time?"

"I like it," Mrs. MacLane said cheerfully, "we keep each other company," and Mrs. Winning felt clumsy and ill-mannered, remembering Mrs. MacLane's widowhood.

As the weather grew warmer and the first signs of green showed on the trees and on the wet ground, Mrs. Winning and Mrs. MacLane became better friends. They met almost daily at the grocery and walked up the hill together, and twice Davey came up to play with Howard's electric train, and once Mrs. MacLane came up to get him and stayed for a cup of coffee in the great kitchen while the boys raced round and round the table and Mrs. Winning's mother-in-law was visiting a neighbor.

"It's such an old house," Mrs. MacLane said, looking up at the dark ceiling. "I love old houses; they feel so secure and warm, as though lots of people had been perfectly satisfied with them and they *knew* how useful they were. You don't get that feeling with a new house."

"This dreary old place," Mrs. Winning said. Mrs. MacLane, with a rose-colored sweater and her bright soft hair, was a spot of color in the kitchen that Mrs. Winning knew she could never duplicate. "I'd give anything in the world to live in your house," Mrs. Winning said.

"*I* love it," Mrs. MacLane said. "I don't think I've ever been so happy. Everyone around here is so nice, and the house is so pretty, and I planted a lot of bulbs yesterday." She laughed. "I used to sit in that apartment in New York and dream about planting bulbs again."

Mrs. Winning looked at the boys, thinking how Howard was half-a-head taller, and stronger, and how Davey was small and weak and loved his mother adoringly. "It's been good for Davey already," she said. "There's color in his cheeks."

"Davey loves it," Mrs. MacLane agreed. Hearing his name Davey came over and put his head in her lap and she touched his hair, bright like her own. "We'd better be getting on home, Davey boy," she said.

"Maybe our flowers have grown some since yesterday," said Davey.

Gradually the days became miraculously long and warm and Mrs. MacLane's garden began to show colors and became an ordered thing, still very young and unsure, but promising rich brilliance for the end of the summer, and the next summer, and summers ten years from now.

"It's even better than I hoped," Mrs. MacLane said to Mrs. Winning, standing at the garden gate. "Things grow so much better here than almost anywhere else."

Davey and Howard played daily after the school was out for the summer, and Howard was free all day. Sometime Howard stayed at Davey's house for lunch, and they planted a vegetable patch together in the MacLane back yard. Mrs. Winning stopped for Mrs. MacLane on her way to the store in the mornings and Davey and Howard frolicked ahead of them down the street. They picked up their mail together and read it walking back up the hill, and Mrs. Winning went more cheerfully back to the big Winning house after walking most of the way home with Mrs. MacLane.

One afternoon Mrs. Winning put the baby in Howard's wagon and with the two boys they went for a long walk in the country. Mrs. MacLane picked Queen Anne's lace and put it into the wagon with the baby, and the boys found a garter snake and tried to bring it home. On the way up the hill Mrs. MacLane helped pull the wagon with the baby and the Queen Anne's lace, and they stopped halfway to rest and Mrs. MacLane said, "Look, I believe you can see my garden all the way from here."

It was a spot of color almost at the top of the hill and they stood looking at it while the baby threw the Queen Anne's lace out of the wagon. Mrs. MacLane said, "I always want to stop here to look at it," and then, "Who is that *beautiful* child?"

Mrs. Winning looked, and then laughed. "He *is* attractive isn't he," she said. "It's Billy Jones." She looked at him herself, carefully, trying to see him as Mrs. MacLane would. He was a boy about twelve, sitting quietly on a wall across the street, with his chin in his hands, silently watching Davey and Howard.

"He's like a young statue," Mrs. MacLane said. "So brown, and will you look at that face?" She started to walk again to see him more clearly, and Mrs. Winning followed her. "Do I know his mother and fath—?"

"The Jones children are half-Negro," Mrs. Winning said hastily. "But they're all beautiful children; you should see the girl. They live just outside town."

Howard's voice reached them clearly across the summer air. "Nigger," he was saying, "nigger, nigger boy."

"Nigger," Davey repeated, giggling.

Mrs. MacLane gasped, and then said, *"Davey,"* in a voice that made Davey turn his head apprehensively; Mrs. Winning had never heard her friend use such a voice, and she too watched Mrs. Mac-Lane.

"Davey," Mrs. MacLane said again, and Davey approached slowly. "What did I hear you say?"

"Howard," Mrs. Winning said, "leave Billy alone."

"Go tell that boy you're sorry," Mrs. MacLane said. "Go at once and tell him you're sorry."

Davey blinked tearfully at his mother and then went to the curb and called across the street, "I'm sorry."

Howard and Mrs. Winning waited uneasily, and Billy Jones across the street raised his head from his hands and looked at Davey and then, for a long time, at Mrs. MacLane. Then he put his chin on his hands again.

Suddenly Mrs. MacLane called, "Young man—Will you come here a minute, please?"

Mrs. Winning was surprised, and stared at Mrs. MacLane, but when the boy across the street did not move Mrs. Winning said sharply, "Billy! Billy Jones! Come here at once!"

The boy raised his head and looked at them, and then slid slowly down from the wall and started across the street. When he was across the street and about five feet from them he stopped, waiting.

"Hello," Mrs. MacLane said gently, "what's your name?"

The boy looked at her for a minute and then at Mrs. Winning, and Mrs. Winning said, "He's Billy Jones. Answer when you're spoken to, Billy."

"Billy," Mrs. MacLane said, "I'm sorry my little boy called you a name, but he's very little and he doesn't always know what he's saying. But he's sorry, too."

"Okay," Billy said, still watching Mrs. Winning. He was wearing an old pair of blue jeans and a torn white shirt, and he was barefoot. His skin and hair were the same color, the golden shade of a very heavy tan, and his hair curled lightly; he had the look of a garden statue.

"Billy," Mrs. MacLane said, "how would you like to come and work for me? Earn some money?"

"Sure," Billy said.

"Do you like gardening?" Mrs. MacLane asked. Billy nodded soberly. "Because," Mrs. MacLane went on enthusiastically, "I've been needing someone to help me with my garden, and it would be just the thing for you to do." She waited a minute and then said, "Do you know where I live?"

"Sure," Billy said. He turned his eyes away from Mrs. Winning and for a minute looked at Mrs. MacLane, his brown eyes expressionless. Then he looked back at Mrs. Winning, who was watching Howard up the street.

"Fine," Mrs. MacLane said. "Will you come tomorrow?"

"Sure," Billy said. He waited for a minute, looking from Mrs. MacLane to Mrs. Winning, and then ran back across the street and vaulted over the wall where he had been sitting. Mrs. MacLane watched him admiringly. Then she smiled at Mrs. Winning and gave the wagon a tug to start it up the hill again. They were nearly at the MacLane cottage before Mrs MacLane finally spoke. "I just can't stand that," she said, "to hear children attacking people for things they can't help."

"They're strange people, the Joneses," Mrs. Winning said readily. "The father works around as a handyman; maybe you've seen him. You see—" she dropped her voice—"the mother was white, a girl from around here. A local girl," she said again, to make it more clear to a foreigner. "She left the whole litter of them when Billy was about two, and went off with a white man."

"Poor children," Mrs. MacLane said.

"*They're* all right," Mrs. Winning said. "The church takes care of them, of course, and people are always giving them things. The girl's old enough to work now, too. She's sixteen, but . . . ."

"But what?" Mrs. MacLane said, when Mrs. Winning hesitated.

"Well, people talk about her a lot, you know," Mrs. Winning said. "Think of her mother, after all. And there's another boy, couple of years older than Billy."

They stopped in front of the MacLane cottage and Mrs. MacLane touched Davey's hair. "Poor unfortunate child," she said.

"Children *will* call names," Mrs. Winning said. "There's not much you can do."

"Well . . ." Mrs. MacLane said. "Poor child."

The next day, after the dinner dishes were washed, and while Mrs. Winning and her mother-in-law were putting them away, the elder

Mrs. Winning said casually, "Mrs. Blake tells me your friend Mrs. MacLane was asking around the neighbors how to get hold of the Jones boy."

"She wants someone to help in the garden, I think," Mrs. Winning said weakly. "She needs help in that big garden."

"Not *that* kind of help," the elder Mrs. Winning said. "You tell her about them?"

"She seemed to feel sorry for them," Mrs. Winning said, from the depths of the pantry. She took a long time settling the plates in even stacks in order to neaten her mind. She *shouldn't* have done it, she was thinking, but her mind refused to tell her why. She should have asked me first, though, she thought finally.

The next day Mrs. Winning stopped off at the cottage with Mrs. MacLane after coming up the hill from the store. They sat in the yellow kitchen and drank coffee, while the boys played in the back yard. While they were discussing the possibilities of hammocks between the apple trees there was a knock at the kitchen door and when Mrs. MacLane opened it she found a man standing there, so that she said, "Yes?" politely, and waited.

"Good morning," the man said. He took off his hat and nodded his head at Mrs. MacLane. "Billy told me you was looking for someone to work your garden," he said.

"Why . . ." Mrs. MacLane began, glancing sideways uneasily at Mrs. Winning.

"I'm Billy's father," the man said. He nodded his head toward the back yard and Mrs. MacLane saw Billy Jones sitting under one of the apple trees, his arms folded in front of him, his eyes on the grass at his feet.

"How do you do," Mrs. MacLane said inadequately.

"Billy told me you said for him to come work your garden," the man said. "Well, now, I think maybe a summer job's too much for a boy his age, he ought to be out playing in the good weather. And that's the kind of work I do anyway, so's I thought I'd just come over and see if you found anyone yet."

He was a big man, very much like Billy, except that where Billy's hair curled only a little, his father's hair curled tightly, with a line around his head where his hat stayed constantly and where Billy's skin was a golden tan, his father's skin was darker, almost bronze. When he moved, it was gracefully, like Billy, and his eyes were the same fathomless brown. "Like to work this garden," Mr. Jones said, looking around. "Could be a mighty nice place."

"You were very nice to come," Mrs. MacLane said. "I certainly do need help."

Mrs. Winning sat silently, not wanting to speak in front of Mr. Jones. She was thinking, I wish she'd ask me first, this is impossible . . . and Mr. Jones stood silently, listening courteously, with his dark eyes on Mrs. MacLane while she spoke. "I guess a lot of the work would be too much for a boy like Billy," she said. "There are a lot of things I can't even do myself, and I was sort of hoping I could get someone to give me a hand."

"That's fine, then," Mr. Jones said. "Guess I can manage most of it," he said, and smiled.

"Well," Mrs. MacLane said, "I guess that's all settled, then. When do you want to start?"

"How about right now?" he said.

"Grand," Mrs. MacLane said enthusiastically, and then, "Excuse me for a minute," to Mrs. Winning over her shoulder. She took down her gardening gloves and wide straw hat from the shelf by the door. "Isn't it a lovely day?" she asked Mr. Jones as she stepped out into the garden while he stood back to let her pass.

"You go along home now, Bill," Mr. Jones called as they went toward the side of the house.

"Oh, why not let him stay?" Mrs. MacLane said. Mrs. Winning heard her voice going on as they went out of sight. "He can play around the garden, and he'd probably enjoy . . ."

For a minute Mrs. Winning sat looking at the garden, at the corner around which Mr. Jones had followed Mrs. MacLane, and then Howard's face appeared around the side of the door and he said, "Hi, is it nearly time to eat?"

"Howard," Mrs. Winning said quietly, and he came in through the door and came over to her. "It's time for you to run along home," Mrs. Winning said. "I'll be along in a minute."

Howard started to protest, but she added, "I want you to go right away. Take my bag of groceries if you think you can carry it."

Howard was impressed by her conception of his strength, and he lifted down the bag of groceries; his shoulders, already broad out of proportion, like his father's and his grandfather's, strained under the weight, and then he steadied on his feet. "Aren't I strong?" he asked exultantly.

"*Very* strong," Mrs. Winning said. "Tell Grandma I'll be right up. I'll just say good-bye to Mrs. MacLane."

Howard disappeared through the house; Mrs. Winning heard him walking heavily under the groceries, out through the open front door and down the steps. Mrs. Winning rose and was standing by the kitchen door when Mrs. MacLane came back.

"You're not ready to go?" Mrs. MacLane exclaimed when she saw Mrs. Winning with her jacket on. "Without finishing your coffee?"

"I'd better catch Howard," Mrs. Winning said. "He ran along ahead."

"I'm sorry I left you like that," Mrs. MacLane said. She stood in the doorway beside Mrs. Winning, looking out into the garden. "How *wonderful* it all is," she said, and laughed happily.

They walked together through the house; the blue curtains were up by now, and the rug with the touch of blue in the design was on the floor.

"Good-bye," Mrs. Winning said on the front steps.

Mrs. MacLane was smiling, and following her look Mrs. Winning turned and saw Mr. Jones, his shirt off and his strong back shining in the sun as he bent with a scythe over the long grass at the side of the house. Billy lay nearby, under the shade of the bushes; he was playing with a grey kitten. "I'm going to have the finest garden in town," Mrs. MacLane said proudly.

"You won't have him working here past today, will you?" Mrs. Winning asked. "Of course you won't have him any longer than just today?"

"But surely—" Mrs. MacLane began, with a tolerant smile, and Mrs. Winning, after looking at her for an incredulous minute, turned and started, indignant and embarrassed, up the hill.

Howard had brought the groceries safely home and her mother-in-law was already setting the table.

"Howard says you sent him home from MacLane's," her mother-in-law said, and Mrs. Winning answered briefly, "I thought it was getting late."

The next morning when Mrs. Winning reached the cottage on her way down to the store she saw Mr. Jones swinging the scythe expertly against the side of the house, and Billy Jones and Davey sitting on the front steps watching him. "Good morning, Davey," Mrs. Winning called, "is your mother ready to go downstreet?"

"Where's Howard?" Davey asked, not moving.

"He stayed home with his grandma today," Mrs. Winning said brightly. "Is your mother ready?"

"She's making lemonade for Billy and me," Davey said. "We're going to have it in the garden."

"Then tell her," Mrs. Winning said quickly, "tell her that I said I was in a hurry and that I had to go on ahead. I'll see her later." She hurried on down the hill.

In the store she met Mrs. Harris, a lady whose mother had worked for the elder Mrs. Winning nearly forty years before. "Helen," Mrs. Harris said, "you get greyer every year. You ought to stop all this running around."

Mrs. Winning, in the store without Mrs. MacLane for the first time in weeks, smiled shyly and said that she guessed she needed a vacation.

"Vacation!" Mrs. Harris said. "Let that husband of yours do the housework for a change. He doesn't have nuthin' else to do."

She laughed richly, and shook her head. "Nuthin' else to do," she said. "The Winnings!"

Before Mrs. Winning could step away Mrs. Harris added, her laughter penetrated by a sudden sharp curiosity: "Where's that dressed-up friend of yours get to? Usually downstreet together, ain't you?"

Mrs. Winning smiled courteously, and Mrs. Harris said, laughing again, "Just couldn't believe those shoes of hers, first time I seen them. Them shoes!"

While she was laughing again Mrs. Winning escaped to the meat counter and began to discuss the potentialities of pork shoulder earnestly with the grocer. Mrs. Harris only says what everyone else says, she was thinking, are they talking like that about Mrs. MacLane? Are they laughing at her? When she thought of Mrs. MacLane she thought of the quiet house, the soft colors, the mother and son in the garden; Mrs. MacLane's shoes were green and yellow platform sandals, odd-looking certainly next to Mrs. Winning's solid white oxfords, but so inevitably right for Mrs. MacLane's house, and her garden . . . . Mrs. Harris came up behind her and said, laughing again, "What's she got, that Jones fellow working for her now?"

When Mrs. Winning reached home, after hurrying up the hill past the cottage, where she saw no one, her mother-in-law was waiting for her in front of the house, watching her come the last few yards. "Early enough today," her mother-in-law said. "MacLane out of town?"

Resentful, Mrs. Winning said only, "Mrs. Harris nearly drove me out of the store, with her jokes."

"Nothing wrong with Lucy Harris getting away from that man of hers wouldn't cure," the elder Mrs. Winning said. Together, they began to walk around the house to the back door. Mrs. Winning, as they walked, noticed that the grass under the trees had greened up nicely, and that the nasturtiums beside the house were bright.

"I've got something to say to you, Helen," the elder Mrs. Winning said finally.

"Yes," her daughter-in-law said.

"It's the MacLane girl, about her, I mean. You know her so well, you ought to talk to her about that colored man working there."

"I suppose so," Mrs. Winning said.

"You *sure* you told her? You told her about those people?"

"I told her," Mrs. Winning said.

"He's there every blessed day," her mother-in-law said. "And working out there without his shirt on. He goes in the house."

And that evening Mr. Burton, next-door neighbor to Mrs. Mac-Lane, dropped in to see the Howard Winnings about getting a new lot of shingles at the mill; he turned suddenly, to Mrs. Winning, who was sitting sewing next to her mother-in-law at the table in the front room, and raised his voice a little when he said, "Helen, I wish you'd tell your friend Mrs. MacLane to keep that kid of hers out of my vegetables."

"Davey?" Mrs. Winning said involuntarily.

"No," Mr. Burton said, while all the Winnings looked at the younger Mrs. Winning, "no, the other one, the colored boy. He's been running loose through our back yard. Makes me sort of mad, that kid coming and spoiling other people's property. You know," he added, turning to the Howard Winnings, "you know, that does make a person mad." There was a silence, and then Mr. Burton added, rising heavily, "Guess I'll say good-night to you people."

They all attended him to the door and came back to their work in silence. I've got to do something, Mrs. Winning was thinking, pretty soon they'll stop coming to me first, they'll tell someone else to speak to *me.* She looked up, found her mother-in-law looking at her, and they both looked down quickly.

Consequently Mrs. Winning went to the store the next morning earlier than usual, and she and Howard crossed the street just above the MacLane house, and went down the hill on the other side.

"Aren't we going to see Davey?" Howard asked once, and Mrs. Winning said carelessly, "Not today, Howard. Maybe your father will take you out to the mill this afternoon."

She avoided looking across the street at the MacLane house, and hurried to keep up with Howard.

Mrs. Winning met Mrs. MacLane occasionally after that at the store or the post office, and they spoke pleasantly. When Mrs. Winning passed the cottage after the first week or so, she was no longer embarrassed about going by, and even looked at it frankly once or twice. The garden was going beautifully; Mr. Jone's broad back was usually visible through the bushes, and Billy Jones sat on the steps or lay on the grass with Davey.

One morning on her way down the hill Mrs. Winning heard a conversation between Davey MacLane and Billy Jones; they were in the bushes together and she heard Davey's high familiar voice saying, "Billy, you want to build a house with me today?"

"Okay," Billy said. Mrs. Winning slowed her steps a little to hear.

"We'll build a big house out of branches," Davey said excitedly, "and when it's finished we'll ask my mommy if we can have lunch out there."

"You can't build a house just out of branches," Billy said. "You ought to have wood, and boards."

"And chairs and tables and dishes," Davey agreed. "And walls."

"Ask your mommy can we have two chairs out here," Billy said. "Then we can pretend the whole garden is our house."

"And I'll get us some cookies, too," Davey said. "And we'll ask my mommy and your daddy to come in our house." Mrs. Winning heard them shouting as she went down along the sidewalk.

You have to admit, she told herself as though she were being strictly just, you have to admit that he's doing a lot with that garden; it's the prettiest garden on the street. And Billy acts as though he had as much right there as Davey.

As the summer wore on into long hot days undistinguishable one from another, so that it was impossible to tell with any real accuracy whether the light shower had been yesterday or the day before, the Winnings moved out into their yard to sit after supper, and in the warm darkness Mrs. Winning sometimes found an opportunity of sitting next to her husband so that she could touch his arm; she was never able to teach Howard to run to her and put his head in her lap, or inspire him with other than the perfunctory Winning affection, but she consoled herself with the thought that at least they were a family, a solid respectable thing.

The hot weather kept up, and Mrs. Winning began to spend more time·in the store, postponing the long aching walk up the hill in the sun. She stopped and chatted with the grocer, with other young mothers in the town, with older friends of her mother-in-law's, talking about the weather, the reluctance of the town to put in a decent swimming pool, the work that had to be done before school started in the fall, chickenpox, the P.T.A. One morning she met Mrs. Burton in the store, and they spoke of their husbands, the heat, and the hot-weather occupations of their children before Mrs. Burton said: "By the way, Johnny will be six on Saturday and he's having a birthday party; can Howard come?"

"Wonderful," Mrs. Winning said, thinking, His good white shorts, the dark blue shirt, a carefully-wrapped present.

"Just about eight children," Mrs. Burton said, with the loving carelessness mothers use in planning the birthday parties of their children. "They'll stay for supper, of course—send Howard down about three-thirty."

"That sounds so nice," Mrs. Winning said. "He'll be delighted when I tell him."

"I thought I'd have them all play outdoors most of the time," Mrs. Burton said. "In this weather. And then perhaps a few games indoors, and supper. Keep it simple—*you* know." She hesitated, running her finger around and around the top rim of a can of coffee. "Look," she said, "I hope you won't mind me asking, but would it be all right with you if I didn't invite the MacLane boy?"

Mrs. Winning felt sick for a minute, and had to wait for her voice to even out before she said lightly, "It's all right with me if it's all right with *you;* why do you have to ask *me?*"

Mrs. Burton laughed. "I just thought you might mind if he didn't come."

Mrs. Winning was thinking, something bad has happened, somehow people think they know something about me that they won't say, they all pretend it's nothing, but this never happened to me before; I live with the Winnings, don't I? "Really," she said, putting the weight of the old Winning house into her voice, "why in the *world* would it bother me?" Did I take it too seriously, she was wondering, did I seem too anxious, should I have let it go?

Mrs. Burton was embarrassed, and she set the can of coffee down on the shelf and began to examine the other shelves studiously. "I'm sorry I mentioned it at all," she said.

Mrs. Winning felt that she had to say something further, something to state her position with finality, so that no longer would Mrs. Burton, at least, dare to use such a tone to a Winning, presume to preface a question with "I hope you don't mind me asking." "After all," Mrs. Winning said carefully, weighing the words, "she's like a second mother to Billy."

Mrs. Burton, turning to look at Mrs. Winning for confirmation, grimaced and said, "Good Lord, Helen!"

Mrs. Winning shrugged and then smiled and Mrs. Burton smiled and then Mrs. Winning said, "I do feel so sorry for the little boy, though."

Mrs. Burton said, "Such a sweet little thing, too."

Mrs. Winning had just said, "He and Billy are together *all* the time now," when she looked up and saw Mrs. MacLane regarding her from the end of the aisle of shelves; it was impossible to tell whether she had heard them or not. For a minute Mrs. Winning looked steadily back at Mrs. MacLane, and then she said, with just the right note of cordiality, "Good morning, Mrs. MacLane Where is your little boy this morning?"

"Good morning, Mrs. Winning," Mrs. MacLane said, and moved on past the aisle of shelves, and Mrs. Burton caught Mrs. Winning's arm and made a desperate gesture of hiding her face and, unable to help themselves, both she and Mrs. Winning began to laugh.

Soon after that, although the grass in the Winning yard under the maple trees stayed smooth and green, Mrs. Winning began to notice in her daily trips past the cottage that Mrs. MacLane's garden was suffering from the heat. The flowers wilted under the morning sun, and no longer stood up fresh and bright; the grass was browning slightly and the rose bushes Mrs. MacLane had put in so optimistically were noticeably dying. Mr. Jones seemed always cool, working steadily; sometimes bent down with his hands in the earth, sometimes tall against the side of the house, setting up a trellis or pruning a tree, but the blue curtains hung lifelessly at the windows. Mrs. MacLane still smiled at Mrs. Winning in the store, and then one day they met at the gate of Mrs. MacLane's garden and after hesitating for a minute, Mrs. MacLane said, "Can you come in for a few minutes? I'd like to have a talk, if you have time."

"Surely," Mrs. Winning said courteously, and followed Mrs. Mac-Lane up the walk, still luxuriously bordered with flowering bushes, but somehow disenchanted, as though the summer heat had baked away the vivacity from the ground. In the familiar living-room Mrs. Winning sat down on a straight chair, holding herself politely stiff, while Mrs. MacLane sat as usual in her armchair.

"How is Davey?" Mrs. Winning asked finally, since Mrs. Mac-Lane did not seem disposed to start any conversation.

"He's very well," Mrs. MacLane said, and smiling as she always did when speaking of Davey. "He's out back with Billy.'

There was a quiet minute, and then Mrs. MacLane said, staring at the blue bowl on the coffe table, "What I wanted to ask you is, what on earth is gone wrong?"

Mrs. Winning had been holding herself stiff in readiness for some such question, and when she said, "I don't know what you mean," she thought, I sound exactly like Mother Winning, and realized, I'm enjoying this, just as *she* would; and no matter what she thought of herself she was unable to keep from adding, "*Is* something wrong?"

"Of course," Mrs. MacLane said. She stared at the blue bowl, and said slowly, "When I first came, everyone was so nice, and they seemed to like Davey and me and want to help us."

That's wrong, Mrs. Winning was thinking, you mustn't ever talk about whether people like you, that's bad taste.

"And the garden was going so well," Mrs. MacLane said helplessly. "And now, no one ever does more than just speak to us—I used to say 'Good morning' over the fence to Mrs. Burton, and she'd come to the fence and we'd talk about the garden, and now she just says, 'Morning' and goes in the house—and no one ever smiles, or anything."

This is dreadful, Mrs. Winning thought, this is childish, this is complaining. People treat you as you treat them, she thought; she wanted desperately to go over and take Mrs. MacLane's hand and ask her to come back and be one of the nice people again; but she only sat straighter in the chair and said, "I'm sure you must be mistaken. I've never heard anyone speak of it."

"*Are* you sure?" Mrs. MacLane turned and looked at her. "Are you sure it isn't because of Mr. Jones working here?"

Mrs. Winning lifted her chin a little higher and said, "Why on earth would anyone around here be rude to you because of Jones?"

Mrs. MacLane came with her to the door, both of them planning vigorously for the days some time next week, when they would all go swimming, when they would have a picnic, and Mrs. Winning went down the hill thinking, The nerve of her, trying to blame the colored folks.

Toward the end of the summer there was a bad thunderstorm, breaking up the prolonged hot spell. It raged with heavy wind and rain over the town all night, sweeping without pity through the trees, pulling up young bushes and flowers ruthlessly; a barn was struck on one side of the town, the wires pulled down on another. In the morning Mrs. Winning opened the back door to find the Winning yard littered with small branches from the maples, the grass bent almost flat to the ground.

Her mother-in-law came to the door behind her. "Quite a storm," she said, "did it wake you?"

"I woke up once and went to look at the children," Mrs. Winning said. "It must have been about three o'clock."

"I was up later," her mother-in-law said. "I looked at the children too; they were both asleep."

They turned together and went in to start breakfast.

Later in the day Mrs. Winning started down to the store; she had almost reached the MacLane cottage when she saw Mrs. MacLane standing in the front garden with Mr. Jones standing beside her and Billy Jones with Davey in the shadows of the front porch. They were all looking silently at a great branch from one of the Burtons' trees that lay across the center of the garden, crushing most of the flowering bushes and pinning down what was to have been a glorious tulip bed. As Mrs. Winning stopped, watching, Mrs. Burton came out on to her front porch to survey the storm-damage, and Mrs. MacLane called to her, "Good morning, Mrs. Burton, it looks like we have part of your tree over here."

"Looks so," Mrs. Burton said, and she went back into her house and closed the door flatly.

Mrs .Winning watched while Mrs. MacLane stood quietly for a minute. Then she looked up at Mr. Jones almost hopefully and she and Mr. Jones looked at one another for a long time. Then Mrs. MacLane said, her clear voice carrying lightly across the air washed clean by the storm: "Do you think I ought to give it up, Mr. Jones? Go back to the city where I'll never have to see another garden?"

Mr. Jones shook his head despondently, and Mrs. MacLane, her shoulders tired, went slowly over and sat on her front steps and

Davey came and sat next to her. Mr. Jones took hold of the great branch angrily and tried to move it, shaking it and pulling until his shoulders tensed with the strength he was bringing to bear, but the branch only gave slightly and stayed, clinging to the garden.

"Leave it alone, Mr. Jones," Mrs. MacLane said finally. "Leave it for the next people to move!"

But still Mr. Jones pulled against the branch, and then suddenly Davey stood up and cried out, "There's Mrs. Winning! Hi, Mrs. Winning!"

Mrs. MacLane and Mr. Jones both turned, and Mrs. MacLane waved and called out, "Hello!"

Mrs. Winning swung around without speaking and started, with great dignity, back up the hill toward the old Winning house.

Kardiner & Ovesey

were in the Departments of Psychiatry and Sociology, Columbia University, when they made the study which was published as *Mark of Oppression*. Dr. Kardiner, a practicing psychiatrist, is the author of *The Individual and His Society* and with associates, *The Psychological Frontiers of Society*.

Psychodynamic inventory

A PSYCHODYNAMIC summary of the findings on twenty-five cases is a very different story from a statistical study of incidence. The psychodynamic composite picture records incidence also, but incidence of patterns of intrapsychic accommodation. Whereas the study of employment vicissitudes in the same number would be totally without significance if it were treated as a sample of what transpired in fourteen million people, the corresponding study in patterns of intrapsychic accommodation has a much higher range of validity. It is doubtful whether we could get much more out of the study of fifty or one hundred cases. The real handicap of studying a small number intensively is not that our findings are unlikely to be representative, but that their representability takes too little account of characterological and vocational differences. This is the trouble with any pilot study. We cannot tell from our studies what comprises the personal adaptation of the successful Negro businessman, the successful actress, the successful baseball player, the successful racketeer, and the like. On the other hand, how important is it for us, in trying to establish a composite picture of Negro adaptation, to include these types of character, who are statistically unimportant, because they are the exceptions and not the rule?

We do not believe that this issue of representability is the most important issue that concerns us. There are other much more troublesome features which will emerge in the course of this summary. There is the question whether caste or class is the dominant Negro source of conflict, and whether the conflicts about caste are so prominent that they submerge differences that would otherwise arise from class distinctions, as is likely to be the case with whites. In this study, we cannot avoid the conclusion that the dominant conflicts of the Negro are created by the caste situation, and that those of class are secondary. This is due to the fact that the adaptation of the Negro is qualified primarily by the color of his skin—an arbitrary but effective line of demarcation.

At best, the question of representability of our findings is secondary to another more important issue. Namely, in what form shall we describe the various kinds of adaptational variations? This opens the whole question of characterology and the study of personality functioning and modes of adaptation generally. To this we can only say that psychodynamics is not the only way that it can be done. It has the limitation of studying adaptation from the point of view of effectiveness and ineffectiveness. It is not tied to any absolutes or archetypes. It has the advantage of having been the subject of experimental verification for over sixty years by many people, and of being internally consistent. We have heard objections of an academic kind that what is described here is not "personality" at all but something else; but we have never heard of any substitutes for describing the vicissitudes of adaptation that do not include the successful or unsuccessful modes of handling life situations. Let those who object supply us with a better frame of reference.

It is a consistent feature of human personality that it tends to become organized about the main problems of adaptation, and this main problem tends to polarize all other aspects of adaptation toward itself. This central problem of Negro adaptation is oriented toward the discrimination he suffers and the consequences of this discrimination for the self-referential aspects of his social orientation. In simple words, it means that his self-esteem suffers (which is self-referential) because he is constantly receiving an unpleasant image of himself from the behavior of others to him. This is the subjective impact of social discrimination, and it sounds as though its effects ought to be localized and limited in influence. This is not the case. It seems to be an ever-present and unrelieved irritant. Its influence is not alone due to the fact that it is painful in its intensity, but also because the individual, in order to maintain internal balance and to protect himself from being overwhelmed by it, must initiate restitutive maneuvers in order to keep functioning—all quite automatic and unconscious. In addition to maintaining an internal balance, the individual must continue to maintain a social façade and some kind of adaptation to the offending stimuli so that he can preserve some social effectiveness. All of this requires a constant preoccupation, notwithstanding the fact that these adaptational processes all take place on a low order of awareness. The following is a diagram of a typical parallelogram of forces:
In the center of this adaptational scheme stand the low self-esteem (the self-referential part) and the aggression (the reactive part). The rest are maneuvers with these main constellations, to prevent their

manifestation, to deny them and the sources from which they come, to make things look different from what they are, to replace aggressive activity which would be socially disastrous with more acceptable ingratiation and passivity. Keeping this system going means, however, being constantly ill at ease, mistrustful, and lacking in confidence. The entire system prevents the affectivity of the individual that might otherwise be available from asserting itself.

This is the adaptational range that is prescribed by the caste situation. This is, however, only a skeletal outline. Many types of elaboration are possible, particularly along projective or compensatory lines. For example, the low self-esteem can be projected as follows:

Low self-esteem = self-contempt → idealization of the white → frantic efforts to be white

$$= \text{unattainable} \nearrow \begin{array}{l} \text{hostility to whites} \\ \searrow \text{introjected white ideal} \rightarrow \end{array}$$

self-hatred → projected on to other Negroes = hatred of Negroes.

The low self-esteem can also mobilize compensations in several forms: (1) apathy, (2) hedonism, (3) living for the moment, (4) criminality.

The disposition of aggression is similarly susceptible to elaboration. The conspicuous feature of rage lies in the fact that it is an emotion that primes the organism for motor expression. Hate is an attenuated form of rage, and is the emotion toward those who inspire fear and rage. The difficult problem for those who are constantly subject to frustration is how to contain this emotion and prevent its motor expression. The chief motive for the latter is to avoid setting in motion retaliatory aggression.

The most immediate effect of rage is, therefore, to set up a fear of its consequences. Fear and rage become almost interchangeable. When the manifestations of rage are continually suppressed, ultimately the individual may cease to be aware of the emotion. In some subjects the *only* manifestation of rage may be fear.

The techniques for disposing of rage are varied. The simplest disposition is to suppress it and replace it with another emotional attitude—submission or compliance. The greater the rage, the more abject the submission. Thus, scraping and bowing, compliance and ingratiation may actually be indicators of suppressed rage and sustained hatred. Rage can be kept under control but replaced with an attenuated but sustained feeling—resentment. It may be kept under control, but ineffectively, and show itself in irritability. It may be kept under sustained control for long periods, and then become explosive. Rage may show itself in subtle forms of ingratiation for purposes of exploitation. It may finally be denied altogether (by an automatic process) and replaced by an entirely different kind of expression, like laughter, gaiety, or flippancy.

Rage may ricochet back on its author, as it does in some types of pain-dependent behavior (masochism). This is only likely to happen when rage is directed toward an object that is loved; the rage is then accompanied by strong guilt feelings. In this case the only manifestation of rage may be depression.

The tensions caused by suppressed or repressed aggression often express themselves through psychosomatic channels. Headaches of the migrainous variety are often the expression of rage which is completely repressed. These are usually not accompanied by amorphous anxiety—though the latter may be the sole vehicle for this aggression. Hypertension is another psychosomatic expression of the same, but predominantly suppressive, process.

In the case histories, we found all these varieties of the expression and control of rage. All kinds of combinations are possible. The two commonest end products of sustained attempts to contain and control aggression were low self-esteem and depression. These are merely the results of the continuous failure of a form of self-assertion:

The adaptational scheme we have charted above takes in the impact of discrimination but does not account for the integrative systems due to other conditions operative in the process of growth. This division is purely arbitrary for actually both series run concomitantly. There is no time in the life of the Negro that he is not actively in contact with the caste situation. The other personality traits derive, however, from the disturbances in his family life. This source gives rise to the following constellations: the affectivity range, the capacity for idealization and ideal formation, the traits derived from reactions to discipline, and conscience mechanisms. In these categories there is some difference as we proceed from the lower- to the upper-class Negro. Let us take up the lower-class Negro first.

Affectivity range means the range of emotional potential. In appraising the role of emotion in personal and social adaptation, we have both quantitative and qualitative features to take into account.

The total adaptation of the individual will depend on how much and what kind of emotion he has in a given situation. Emotion in man's adaptation tends to operate on a mass action principle. That is, the predominance of one emotion tends to stifle all others.

Emotion has the function of orientation toward objects in the outer world that can be the source of frustration or gratifications. The individual responds to a frustrating object with the emergency emotions of fear and rage, and their derivatives of hate, suspicion, distrust, apprehensive anticipation, and the like. These functions are self-preservative in intent and gear the organism for defensive action. The feeling toward objects which are the source of gratifications is the wish to be near, to perpetuate the influence of, to love, to desire, to have anticipations of continued gratifications, to trust, to have confidence, to cooperate with.

We must stress the point from this inventory that the emotions most conducive to social cohesion are those that pertain to the categories of love, trust, and confidence. All creatures are natively endowed with the capacity for fear and rage. The positively toned feelings of love, trust, and confidence, however, must largely be cultivated by eperience. Hence, when we refer to the affectivity potential of an individual, we do not mean the emergency functions of fear and rage. We mean rather the capacity for cooperative and affectionate relatedness to others.

None of these emotions functions in isolation; they have a continuous adaptive interplay during the entire process of growth and living. What counts in the individual are the types of emotional response that become habitual and automatic. These fixed patterns of emotion are not only adaptive, in the sense that they are reaction types to actual situations; they also play a dominant role in shaping anticipations and to a degree, therefore, influence how events will shape up. For example, a person trained to be suspicious will shape the actual events of his life in such a way that his suspicions appear warranted.

The emotions play a decisive role in determining the sociability (peaceful cooperation with others) of the individual through the development of conscience mechanisms and the formation of ideals. The desire on the part of the child to be loved and protected is the dominant incentive for the child to be obedient to his protectors. He needs this because he is helpless himself. The child thus bcomes socialized in order to continue the boons of love and protection. He learns to anticipate the requirements for these returns by internalizing them and making them automatic. He also learns the methods of escaping blame and of devising techniques for reinstatement. Thus, the fear of punishment and the withdrawal of love exert a powerful restraining influence against antisocial behavior. The reward for conformity is a sense of pride in the social recognition of "good" behavior, while the fear of detection and punishment leads to guilty fear and either an anticipation of punishment or self-punishment.

However, in order for these positive emotional feelings and the functions of conscience to be instituted, certain behavior by the parents toward the child is required. Thus, we cannot expect the child to develop affection and dependence on the parent who is not constant in his care, who does not love in return for obedience, whose punishments are either disproportionate, or have no relation to the offense. In this instance, conformity is of no adaptive value at all. A child who is constantly abused by the parent cannot be expected to have pleasant anticipations or to idealize the parent or wish to be like him. A child exposed to this kind of behavior from the parent will not love, trust, or cooperate. It can take flight from the hostile environment and try to seek another more friendly one. Or it can stay and hate the parent, and suppress all the hostile feeling.

On the institutional side, the family structure of the lower-class Negro is the same as the white. However, in the actual process of living, the vicissitudes of the lower-class family are greater and its stability much less. This is where the broken family through early death of parents, abandonment or divorce, takes a heavy toll on the opportunities for developing strong affective ties to the parents. First, the needs for dependency are frustrated. This makes the mother a frustrating object, rather than one the child can depend on. This does not mean that it is the intention of the mothers to neglect or mistreat their children. Quite the contrary, the intention is the usual one, and many lower-class Negro mothers have strong maternal feelings, are exceedingly protective, and try to be good providers. This is not, however, what one hears from the subject. They tell chiefly the story of frustration and of arbitrary discipline by mothers. Not infrequently there is also the constant story of beating and cursing as disciplinary reinforcements. The rivalry situation between siblings in the lower classes is greatly enhanced by the general scarcity in which they live. This situation, of course, is greatly magnified when the child is given to some other relative for custody, as a consequence of a broken home. These children fare worse than any of the others. They are the ones who, because of mistreatment, decide at the age of 10 or 12 to run away and shift for themselves. In these children, some of whom we studied, the premature independence hardly works to the advantage of the personality in the long run. They become shrewd and adjustable, but at the cost of complete mistrust in everyone.

The result of the continuous frustrations in childhood is to create a personality devoid of confidence in human relations, of an eternal vigilance and distrust of others. This is a purely defensive maneuver which purports to protect the individual against the repeatedly traumatic effects of disappointment and frustration. He must operate on the assumption that the world is hostile. The self-referential aspect of this is contained in the formula "I am not a lovable creature." This, together with the same idea drawn from the caste situation, leads to a reinforcement of the basic destruction of self-esteem.

Thus, many of the efforts of the lower-class Negro at emotional relatedness are canceled out by the inner mistrust in others, the conviction that no one can love him for his own sake, that he is not lovable. Under these conditions, not much real social relatedness is possible. It is, however, very significant that the lower-class Negro is an inveterate "joiner" in one kind of social voluntary organization or another, of clubs and cliques with high-sounding names and with much ritualism in initiation rites. In these organizations, which have a very short life span, there is continuous discord, jockeying for position and prestige, and insistence that each member must have his own way. In other words, through these clubs and associations, the Negro tries to compensate for his lack of relatedness. But for the greater part, he fails. The intrapsychic mistrust and need for dominance destroy the effectiveness of these compensatory efforts. This is a noteworthy feature of Negro life, because the social organizations are supposed to facilitate cooperative endeavor and to give the members the satisfaction of belonging to something, to diminish their isolation. This end is not accomplished because most of the energy of these "associations" is taken up with overcoming mutual distrust and very little energy goes into the mutual supportive aspects of the organization.

Closely related to the question of the affectivity potential is the capacity for idealization. This trait is a general human characteristic, and is rooted in the biological make-up of man. It is the most powerful vehicle for the transmission of culture. During his helpless state man must place his trust in the parent who is his support. If this support and affection aid the individual in his adjustment, the natural tendency is to magnify the powers of the parent to magical proportions. This projection of magical attributes on the parent is the most powerful implement the parent has in enforcing discipline, because the threat of withdrawal of this support creates anxiety in the child. It follows, therefore, that the idealized parent is the satisfying parent whose authority is less enforced than it is delegated, and the acquiescence to discipline is a method the child has for perpetuating those boons he has already enjoyed in the past and hence expects to enjoy in the future.

The formation of ideals to pursue is a corollary of the idealization of the parent. It is easy to identify oneself with the idealized parent if the expectations from him have been realized. If these expectations are frustrated, then there may develop a reactive ideal or the opposite to the one experienced. This is generally a rare phenomenon, where a mistreated child becomes an ideal parent by living the opposite of what he has experienced. It does indeed happen. But it is far from the rule. The commonest outcome of this situation is that despite the hatred to the parent, the child takes on and identifies himself with the hated and frustrating attributes and becomes the replica of the frustrating parent. Here one must draw the line between an activating ideal and the unconscious identification. The activating ideal may be "I will be a provident parent;" the unconscious identification, however, may be with the frustrating parent. In some instances, the mistreated child when it becomes the parent is actuated by the idea: "Why should I give you what I never had myself?" These are the cases in which the frustrated dependency cravings interfere with the protective parental role.

The question of Negro-ideal formation is hardly limited to the parental role. The "ideal" answers the question: "Whom do I want to be like?" This is where the Negro encounters a great deal of difficulty. The parent is a member of a despised and discriminated-against group. Hence, this ideal is already spoiled because it carries with it a guarantee of external and reflected hatred. No one can embrace such an idea. Furthermore, until very recently the Negro has had no real culture heroes (like Joe Louis and Jackie Robinson) with whom he could identify. It is therefore quite natural that the Negro ideal should be *white*. However, accepting the white ideal is a recipe for perpetual self-hatred, frustration, and for tying one's life to unattainable goals. It is a formula for living life on the delusional basis of "as if." The acceptance of the white ideal has acted on the Negro as a slow but cumulative and fatal psychological poison. Its disastrous effects were due to the fact that the more completely he accepted the white ideal, the greater his intrapsychic discomfort had to become. For he could never become *white*. He had, therefore, to settle for the delusion of whiteness through an affectation of white attributes or those that most closely resembled them. This also means the destruction of such native traits as are susceptible to change (kinky hair, etc.). In its most regressive form, this ideal becomes the frantic wish to be reborn white. Pride in oneself could not, therefore, be vested in attributes one had, but in attributes one aspired to have, that is to say, on borrowed ideals. This maneuver, calculated as a restitutive one, ends by being destructive of self-esteem.

The reactions to discipline and the dynamics of conscience mechanisms are closely interrelated, and these in turn are related to the general affectivity potential and ideal formation.

In general, there are several factors operating on the parental side of the induction of disciplines which differ from the situation among whites. The Negro parent has no authority in the social world in which he lives. It is, therefore, a strong temptation for the Negro parent to tend to be authoritative in the only place where he can exercise it, namely in his own home. Hence, we get repeated stories of children being subjected to disciplines that are both arbitrary, instantaneous, and inconsistent, depending often on whim, and at the same time without the ability to offer the child the appropriate rewards for obedience and conformity. Children recognize these rewards chiefly in terms of need satisfactions. These the parent, more often than not, cannot implement. They often fail on the sheer subsistence level. Such a parent cannot have much delegated authority or inspire much dependence. Hence, the authority of the parent is destroyed. A second factor occurs especially in those cases where the mother works. She has no time to be the careful and provident mother. After a day's work, during which time the child often shifts for itself, she is inclined to be tired and irritable which accounts for much of her impatience and insistence on immediate and unqualified obedience.

As between mother and father, many factors conspire to make the mother the chief object of such dependency as is possible under the circumstances. The male as provider and protector definitely suffers disparagement. The mother's objective—since she has so little time—is to make the child as little nuisance as possible. This makes her both an object to be feared and at the same time the only one that can be relied upon.

In passing, we must mention here the place of street life for the Negro child and adolescent. In many ways this street life is no different from corresponding street life in lower-class whites. The crowded home is not a happy place for the growing child, especially when parents are so often away. Since the family does not implement its disciplines with appropriate rewards, the children tend to get their ideals and pattern their amusements on the opportunities of the street, with its values, its heroism, its ideals, and its factionalism. They differ from corresponding white groups in the quantity of the savagery of their mutual aggression, in which the boys get seriously hurt and in some instances killed. Part of this street life pattern is the result of sheer boredom and the irrelevancy of education. Hence, they cannot be attentive at school or get the feeling that they are engaged in a meaningful and ego-enhancing activity. Many of these high school boys have been to bed with women the age of their female teachers and the disciplines and obligations of school life make no sense to them. In consequence, school is treated as a meaningless routine. The street, on the other hand, offers adventure, struggle for dominance, mock and real hostilities. It is, in other words, a better training for life—according to their sights—than education. Delinquency among adolescents runs high for very good reasons.

In this general setting we can evaluate the effects of the socializing disciplines.

We have seen but little evidence of rigid anal training in childhood. There is no serious contest of will between parent and child over this aspect of socialization. It is largely neglected, and in those who came from the South, there was little emphasis on order, neatness, or systematization. Hence, in this group we would not expect much adventitious use of the anal zone for elaborate constellations about expulsion and retention. If there are any compulsive traits in the Negroes of this group, they do not derive from this source.

A more important aspect of socializing discipline is in the sexual domain. Here the picture is very confused. In the lower classes, the sex morality taught is of the Victorian variety. However, there is but little effort made to implement it. There is, on the whole, much less anxiety introduced into sexual disciplines than is the case with the white middle classes. The result is actually more sexual freedom among lower-class Negro children than among whites. And it is by no means unusual for boys and girls to be inducted into sexual activity quite early (7 to 13). It is therefore highly unlikely that potency troubles in both males and females of this group derive from anxieties introduced into the picture by parental threats. In those cases observed these difficulties usually arose from another source. They came from the confusion in the sociosexual roles of male and female. The male derives these difficulties from his inability to assume the effective masculine role according to white ideals, as against the dominant position of the female, first in the dominant mother and later in the dominant wife. The economic independence of the female plays havoc with the conventional male-female roles, and this in turn, influences the potency of the males. In the case of the female, her sociosexual role is reversed. She is dominant, and rebels against the passive and dependent role. Thus, the sexuality of the Negro in the lower classes is confused by the sexual significance of the social role.

Contrary to expectations, the sexual drive of the adult Negro is relatively in abeyance. We saw no evidence of the sex-craved and abandoned Negro. This playing down of sex is the result of the socioeconomic hardship and the confusion in the sexual roles.

What kind of conscience mechanism can be integrated under these conditions? This situation is, if anything, more complex than in the white. Basically, the tonicity of the conscience mechanism depend on the ability of the parent to act as provider of satisfactions. Hence, in the lower-class Negro, we cannot expect strong internalized conscience. If we add to this the disastrous effects of the caste system, then the lower-class Negro, in his hatred for the white, is robbed of any incentive for developing a strong conscience. However, the effects of the caste system are such that they inspire a great deal of fear. Therefore, antisocial tendencies would be held in rigid check by fear of detection. In fact, we can say that conscience in the lower-class Negro is held in tow by his general vigilance over his hatred and aggression, in that the fear of detection of his aggression and antisocial tendencies are both governed by the same mechanisms. The great danger for the lower-class Negro is that these control devices may occasionally and impulsively be overwhelmed—a factor that is of enormous concern to every lower-class Negro.

The group of constellations sets up in the Negro a strong need for compensatory activities, to help establish some semblance of internal harmony. Those compensatory activities have the function of (a) bolstering self-esteem, (b) narcotizing the individual against traumatic impact, (c) disparaging the other fellow, (d) getting magical aid for status improvement.

Among the activities for bolstering self-esteem are flashy and flamboyant dressing, especially in the male, and the denial of Negro attributes, such as doing away with kinky hair.

Narcotizing the individual against traumatic influences is effected largely through alcohol and drugs. In these activities, the males predominate. Alcoholic psychoses in Negroes occur twice the frequency that they do in whites.[1] Narcotics have a wide use among Negroes, but their high cost makes alcohol much more available.

Disparaging the other fellow is widespread among urban Negroes. It is of a vindictive and vituperative kind and drives largely from the status strivings. The street corner and candy store are favorite places for malicious gossip.

In the domain of magical aid to self-esteem, gambling takes a high place. This takes the form of card playing but more often of participation in the numbers racket. Here everyone has a chance at beating fate, of being the favored one, if only for a day. The lure of this tantalizing game must be very high, judging from the vast fortune spent annually by the bulk of the Negro population.

In addition to these, there are occasional outlets, chiefly by males, which stem from their inability to plan or have any confidence in a future. Since the general tendency is to live from day to day, explosive spending when they have money is not infrequent. An occasional illusion of plenty and luxury can thus be created, even if to do so means to mortgage one's energy for months ahead to pay for the luxury.

This psychological picture is to some extent changed in the middle and upper classes. Here the family organization corresponds more closely to the middle-class white group. The emphasis shifts from subsistence problems to status problems. There is also a shift from female to male dominance in the family. The chief conflict area is that concerned with status. In general, the benefits derived from

---

[1] *See* Malzberg, Benjamin, "Mental Disease Among American Negroes: A Statistical Analysis," in Klineberg, Otto (ed.), *Characteristics of the American Negro*, Harper, 1944.

better parental care, better induction of affectivity, better ideal formation and more tonic conscience mechanisms are to a large extent canceled out by the enormous increase in status conflict caused by the caste situation.

In appraising the adaptation of the middle- and upper-class Negro, we encountered a good deal of difficulty in differentiating the real from the apparent. For example, the affectivity potential is much better in this group than in the lower class. But against this we must discount the fact that the representations of better affectivity rest largely on a formal basis. Their marriages are more stable; they induct affectivity more appropriately, etc. But these features are due largely to the fact that the upper- and middle-class Negroes strive hardest to live and feel like the whites. Thy are more conventional, have more rigid sex mores, set more store by "respectability" than do lower-class Negroes. They know what the "right" feelings are for a given situation and they try very hard to have them. But whether they do or do not depends on the quantity of the conflicts they have on the issues of skin color and status strivings, all of which tend to detract from the freedom of feeling.

In the specific integrative areas this group approximates the white. Parental care is good in the same sense and with the same incompatibilities as with whites. The affectivity potential is apparently higher than in lower-class Negroes and they have more capacity for relatedness. They have a high capacity for idealization, but what is idealized is white and not Negro. Here again the ideal formation in the Negro has two layers. The natural figure to idealize is the provident parent; but he is a disparaged figure. Introjecting this object means to hate it to the accompaniment of perpetual guilt. The substitution of a white object as the source of the ideal does not solve the problem. It, too, is hated and likewise must give rise to guilt. The Negro cannot win in either case. As one upper-class Negro observed: "The only thing black that I like is myself." Their ideal formation is of a high order, but founders on the rock of unattainable ideals. The fact that these ideals are relatively more capable of achievement than in the lower classes renders the conflict sharper. Thus, they tend to drive themselvs harder, make greater demands on themselves for accomplishment, and are obligated to refuse the compensatory activities open to lower-class Negroes. This greatly augments the internal self-hatred and makes it more difficult to accept the Negro status. I could love myself "if" is all the more tantalizing because they can almost make the grade, but for skin color. They are therefore more vulnerable to depressd self-esteem than the lower class.

The need to conform to white standards of middle-class respectability gives the upper classes a harder time with their control of aggression. And this in turn has a constricting effect on all their affectivity.

In view of the good parental care, one would expect that their tendencies to passivity would be accentuated. But this is countered by the strong pressure against any form of passivity or subordination especially to other Negroes—since they cannot avoid subordination to the white. This constellation would be very valuable to follow through in Negro homosexuals. As we saw in the biographies, the conflict about passivity in the males was enormous.

The points where the intrapsychic conflicts are sharpened for the middle- and upper-class Negro, then, are in the disposition and compensations for lowered self-esteem, the disposition of aggression, and in the uncompromising acceptance of white ideals.

The self-hatred of this group takes the usual form of projection on both white and on Negroes lower than themselves. However, they have more guilt about their Negro hatred than is the case with lower classes. To the whites, the formula is hatred + control = a disguise; to Negroes the formula is hatred + guilt = anxiety of retaliation. Thus, every middle- and upper-class Negro has increased competitiveness with whites, but his psychological task is merely one of control and concealment. The hatred to the Negro has a way of ricocheting back on its source. Every Negro who is higher than lower class has a sense of guilt to other Negroes because he considers success a betrayal of his group and a piece of aggression against them. Hence, he has freqeuntly what might be called a "success phobia," and occasionally cannot enjoy the fruits of his achievements.

In his acceptance of white ideals, the Negro often overshoots the mark. He overdoes the sex mores so that the incidence of frigidity in the women is very high. In his acceptance of the white man's cleanliness obsession, the Negro ends by identifying himself with feces, and becomes extraordinarily clean and meticulous. However, the obstructions to the accomplishments of white ideals lead to increase in aggression, anxiety, depression of self-esteem, and self-hatred. This compels him to push harder against the social barriers, to drive himself harder, and ends with more frustration and more self-hatred. This vicious circle never ends.

Thus, as we stated above, it is difficult to appraise the advantages and disadvantages of the upper classes as regards their intrapsychic effects. The shift from female to male orientation at least saves this group from the confusion of social and sexual roles. It is one of male dominance and clear definition of sexual role. However, they overdo the rigidity of sexual restrictions, and this affects the female more than the male. The marriages are more stable, but the importance of conventionality is very high; hence the impression remains that as an average the marriages are not more happy. Affectivity is better; but its betterment is largely on the formal side.

The chief outcome of the psychological picture is that the upper classes of Negro society have so much controlling to do of their psychic life, that they must be extremely cramped and constricted and unspontaneous. There is too little self-contentment for true abandonment, and too much self-hatred and mutual mistrust for effective social relatedness. They must constantly choose the lesser evil between spontaneity and getting hurt by retaliation. Hence, they prefer not to see things as they are, or to enter too deeply into anything to the accompaniment of apathy and resignation.

Is there such a thing as a basic personality for the Negro? This work proves decidedly that there is. Though he lives in American culture, the Negro lives under special conditions which give this personality a distinctive configuration. Taking as our base line the white middle class, the conditions of life for the Negro are so distinctive that there is an actual alteration of the pressures to which he must adapt. Hence, he develops a distinctive personality. This basic Negro personality is, however, a caricature of the corresponding white personality, because the Negro must adapt to the same culture, must accept the same social goals, but without the ability to achieve them. This limitation in social opportunities accounts for the difference in personality configuration.

Seymour Krim

one time editor of *Show,* is a critic
and essayist of long standing. Editor
of *Nugget,* he also is a contributor to
Book Week and has edited a collection, *Manhattan* and another, *The
Beats.* He is also the author of *Views
of a Nearsighted Cannoneer.*

Ask for a white cadillac

AFTER I wrote my article on the so-called white hipster and novelty-digging people of every stripe who imitate the Negro's style (*The Village Voice*, October 31, 1957) I came in for biting criticism in Greenwich Village, where I live. Friends of mine, and newly-made enemies as well, accused me of being anti-Negro; the influx of tense, self-conscious, easily-offended Negroes who have recently hit the Village has made any frank statement about colored life extremely delicate and often full of double-jointed guilt feelings; in fact I myself began to have grave doubts as to the truth of what I had written when I saw the reaction.

I now believe (a year and a half later) that my comments were essentially valid—in spite of my own, and every man's limited angle of vision—and therefore of value, since any ounce of truth that can be dug out of the world and placed on the scale of justice wins you a moneyless prize, but one that gives point to your days. To ask for credit for trying to tell the truth, however, is the naïvest kind of romanticism when you finally realize that the balance of life is maintained by cruel necessity. Truth is a bitter mirror to a humanity limping with wounded pride toward the heart's blind castle of contentment; those who would fool with it must be prepared for the worst, for in their zeal they are lancing the most private dreams of the race. After the anger, sentimentality and truly hurt communications that I received after my original piece, I felt compelled to investigate, the whole bruised subject in more depth and background, to search for my own true attitude in relationship to the Negro. More than most white or non-Negro men I have haunted colored society, loved it (and been stomach-kicked by aspects of it), sucked it into my marrow. I aim here to tell as much of the truth about myself in connection with Negroes as I am capable of, with the knowledge that while it will no doubt expose my weaknesses of mind and temperament it will be another small step in destroying the anxiety that makes us try to balance on eggshells and bite our tongues and souls for saying the wrong thing. Complete equality for Negroes (and more subtly, for whites in relation to them) will only come when writers and speakers level down the whole dirty highway of their experience—level all the way.

Having been born in New York City in 1922—Washington Heights, to be exact—the image of the Negro first came to me through jazz and a colored maid (how proud young Negroes must burn at that—I would!) who took care of me as an infant. As to the maid's influence, it is unconscious but surely present; I remember nothing except for the dim feeling of warmth, big soft breasts, perhaps honeyed laughter with the head thrown back in that rich queenly way of buxom Negresses which has been type-cast to death, but is too vital to succumb. But I do recall vividly the beat of jazz rippling through our household from morning until night. My mother played Victor Herbertish light classics on the piano and my father sung them in a proud-peacock way, but my older brother and sister, during the 1920's, got right on board with the new jazz music and the big beat pounded away from both the bedroom (where my brother blew his tenor sax) and the living-room (where my sister edged my mother off the piano seat and made the keys hop). What fascinated me as much as the music itself, even as a boy, was the verbal style that accompanied jazz; the easy, informal play on words that instinctively crept into the voice of people who spoke about or sung jazz. This was a Negro invention quite as much as the music itself, a wonderful, melodic, laughing camp with the hard white words that took the lead out of them and made them swing.

But it was translated into white terms, or middle-class lingo, by the easy-throated, golden-rhythmed Bing Crosby, whose voice dipped and flirted and slurred with great beauty to my 12-year-old ear when he introduced a tune over the radio or played with some lyrics while singing. It always seemed to me that Crosby had a powerful effect on the lovely small-talk of this country, its inflection and casualness, and that this came from The Groaner's being the almost unwitting ("I was a wheel that rolled uphill"—Crosby) ambassador from the black-belt to the white. He dug instinctively and with great fluid taste—in spite of his collegiate front—what lay behind jazz: the good-natured mockery of stiff white manners by Negroes and the sweetening of dry attitudes into rich, flexible, juicy ones.

The Negro to me, then, in my kid-ignorance, was jazz and fun; this was due to the accidents of my personal history—the fact that I came from a Northern, comfortable, Jewish middle-class family and was shielded from any competitive or side-by-side contact with

Negroes. Colored men and women were exotica to me during my childhood, magical, attractive aliens to the normal rhythm of the world. I take no pride in saying this. But because of my background and that of thousands like me, we couldn't know Negroes as the rounded human beings they are but saw them through a particular port-hole of wonder and odd fascination. Unfortunately, Negroes were thought of as being the servant class by people of my economic bracket; but because my family was Jewish and in some way (in others ,not) compassionate because of the endless history of trial of the J's, Negroes were never mistreated in my home. To be fair, however, I have heard numerous Jews from lower economic groups—not to mention people from every other race in America—heap verbal scorn on the *schvatsa*, even at this late date. It goes without saying that such people are bucking for a future red harvest of bloody noses, both for themselves and more thoughtful people.

When I was about 15 the Negro came into my life with a wallop directly connected with the sex drive. It should be no secret that until the war the colored girl was the great underground sex symbol for the U.S. white man, the recipient of his trembling mixture of guilt, leer and male-sadistic desire. Feeling inferior due to what I thought was my physical unattractiveness (where have you heard that before?), I had never been able to make it with the pretty, aggressive Jewish girls of my own environment; not only was I an awkward, fear-haunted, savagely shy kid, my ego had been blasted full of holes by my being orphaned at the age of 10 and my having lived in a state of psychological panic all through my adolescence. I took refuge in heartless masturbation (yes, in technicolor!) and the Negro chick in all her stereotyped, Cotton-Club majesty became my glory-hole for imagined sex bouts of every exciting kind.

There should be nothing shocking in your reading this. Thousands of white American men have done the same, I'm positive, and the reason why they selected Negresses hinges on the double taboo of both sex (long explained and still life's quivering ice-cream) and physical intimacy with a colored person. Together, the behind-the-shed appeal to a *timid* and therefore *prurient* white kid like myself was dynamite. Thus it was that the Negro girl became my jazz queen, someone who loved (in my imagination) to f—k, could never get enough, was supreme physically, rhythmically, ecstatically—"Oh, baby give it to me!" I know only too well that this is a standard cliche and that my blunt picture of it might be offensive; I also know that for historically and psychologically understandable reasons there was, and still is, some truth in this stereotype.

My love of jazz and ranging enslavement to sex came together and focused burningly on the colored girl, but it wasn't until I moved down to the Village—already violently pro-Negro-radical-crudely Whitemanesque—in my early 20's that I first slept with a Negro chick. This baptism was a nothing experience: the girl was Villagey, neurotic, affected, unswinging, among the first of the colored pioneers to make it downtown. In those, my early Village days, she was just one gal among several whom one made and then lost in the merry-go-round of kicks that whirled me and my buddies. Days and nights were lost to us in an almost fanatical pursuit of pleasure during the war-ruptured mid 1940's, with booze, tea (pot), literature, psychiatry and sex leading us headlong into the foam of ever-new experience. But this wild hedonism played itself out in time both for me and my friends. We had to cope with our private selves. Weaknesses in each separated us from the pack, and our lives became more private, secretive, smaller, pettier. Things we had hidden from one another and from ourselves began to obsess us, and I in particular found that I had no genuine confidence toward women and could only make them (or so I thought) by not wearing my glasses and not being myself. I could no longer go on the charm and boyish good looks—as synthetic as not wearing my specs, since I'd had my nose "fixed" when I was 17—that buoyed me up when I first climbed aboard the Village kicks-train. I was becoming lonelier, more introspective, and hung up to the ceiling in my relationships with women. But my hunger for sex (warmth! light! life! the complete holy works!) was as cancerous as ever, and I craved, needed, burned for the gratification. It was then that I first began to go up to Harlem and really see dark society in its own hive.

2

I naturally went to prostitutes in Harlem, but I eased my way into this way of life—for it became that—by enjoying and digging the sights and human scenes of Harlem for their own sake. Here was the paradise of sensuality (to my thirsting eyes) that I had dreamed of for years, but had never gotten to know except for fleeting, half-scared trips through this no-man's land. Now, nerveless because of the heat of my desire (and even when this hot temperature in me waned I never once felt the anxieties on Harlem streets that my white friends tell me is a normal fear) I began to sidle up to my quarry from several sides—listening to jump music from the fine box at the Hotel Theresa bar, seeing the show in the small room at The Baby Grand on 125th St., going to the Friday night stage shows at the Apollo, getting the rhythm and feel of the place by stalking the streets and being perpetually slain within by the natural style of the men, women, and whizzingly precocious kids. Harlem to me, as I got to know it, was a mature wonderland (until I saw the worms behind the scenery). Not only was the sex there for the asking—provided your wallet was full, Jack—but the entire place was a jolt to anybody with a literary or even a human imagination. The streets hummed and jumped with life right out in the open, such a contrast to the hidden, bottled-up phobias that I knew so well. You can't hide your life if you're a poor or scuffling Negro and live frankly among your own people. Jesus, it broke out everywhere, the cripples and amputees I saw begging or laughing or triple-talking someone out of bread (loot) on street-corners; the high heel-crackling (with metal plates so they can be *heard*, man!) sleepless hustling chicks on some money-goal errand in the middle of the afternoon, wearing shades against the enemy day-light and looking hard and scornful of tragedy because they knew it too well; the go-all-night male cats gathering around some modern-istic bar in the late afternoon, freshly pressed and pomaded and ready to shoot the loop on life for the next 20 hours, crap-shooting, card-playing, horse-playing, numbers-running, involved in 15 myste-rious and button-close deals with women—either girls working for them in "the life" (hustling), as I got to say, or sponsoring them in some gambling bit or this or that. The whole teeming place was alive to me in every foot of every block, for there was everywhere a literal acting-out of the needs and desires that all of us are con-demned to cope with until we quit the scene, but here in Harlem there could be no false pride about doing your dirty-work behind a screen. Even when I cooled my sexual heat there many times—in a cellar near a coal-bin, lying on a pallet, or in a room with four other men and women pumping away on three cots barely separated from each other—I felt little or none of the shame I would have had in downtown Manhattan doing the same thing. On the contrary, I began to think that this was more real, natural and human, given the situa-tion of Harlem as I knew it and as people had to live it out to *make* a life for themselves.

I began to feel very much at home uptown—and felt thunderbolt excitement, too. As a writer as well as a frustrated, needy man, I could never get over how Russian the amount of dramatic life I saw was. Here were the same radical contrasts of money and poverty, of tremendous displays of temper and murderous emotion, of hustlers and johns making their arrangements next to funeral parlors where last night's balling stud had perhaps just been laid out. (I obviously mean Russia before the Revolution of 1917.) Humor, the most quick and subtle shafts of wit, shot like sabre-points of Mozartian sparkle across street corners and bars where hostile or drink-angry people were mouthing the favorite Harlem curse for all frustration, "Motherf—ker motherf-king motherf-ker!" And through all of this street-embattled life ran the perpetual beauty of clothes, threads, duds!—bold, high-style dresses and appointments on the girls (flashing jewelry, dyed platinum-blonde hair over a tan face, elbow-length white evening gloves handcuffed with a fake black-onyx bracelet) while the guys were as button-rolled and razor-sharp as hip clotheshorses stepping right out of a showroom. Certainly I saw poor, frayed, styleless people and outfits: but the percentage of sartorial harmony and inventiveness was keener, perhaps out of the need to *impress*, than I had ever seen in any other single New York City community.

In fact I learned about clothes in Harlem—more than I ever had in college or fancy midtown Manhattan, when I worked on *The New Yorker* surrounded by smooth Yale-Princeton-Groton boys. Clothes merely seemed an external decoration to me then, and the pork-pied smoothies often seemed like phantoms with little or no personality. But in Harlem clothes literally make the man and woman: every hair of imagination, flair, nerve, taste, can be woven into your garb, and the tilt of a hat on a hustling, attractive spade cat will be pretty nearly an unerring clue to the style you'll run up against when you speak to him. The girls love a big approach in dress, stagey, rich, striking, and when you consider the color they have to work with you understand the way they'll pour on reds and yellows that smite the eye and make the average white girl seem mousey and drab by comparison. My own style of dress when I first hit Harlem was the casual approach which I wore in the Village and also uptown in the 40's—shined loafers, button-down shirt with a decent, perhaps regimental-stripe tie, a suit jacket and odd slacks (mostly the GI khaki type that can creep by as smart if the crease is truly alive). When I made my opening passes at the whore bars in Harlem—which you get to know by keeping your ears open, following a smile, seeing the number of chicks lined up at the mahogany—I felt embarrassed by my outfit in contrast to the tailor-made cordovan-shoed jazz that the bar-jockeys were showing. My embarrassment was correct to feel, for one or two of the frank hustlers I ran into soon after I made my play—within the first week—wondered "why the hell don't you dress, man?" (I later found out that in Harlem there are three gradations of male dress: clean, pressed, and "dap"—for dapper. Everything can be squeezed into these three categories, and by Harlem standards I was barely clean for any kind of swinging night-life.) After I had been properly put down about my clothes, which were slightly insulting to the dress-tight colored hustling chicks and the sharp male studs, out of misunderstanding, I had to think about drapes in a new way.

I was taught that in Harlem if a man wants to make out with women he has to behave like a man, not a boy or a half-vague intellectual: he has to dress like he knows the score, is not afraid to be bold and flairful in the eyes of women, and wear a slick, capable look about him. Probably Negroes who have scored with money uptown wear the insignia of it on their back as a sign of pride or superiority; certainly some of it is narcissistic strutting and over-obvious, but in a rough community like Harlem there is nothing wrong in proving who and what you are by your appearance. You can't be a self-effacing Shelley or a Chopin—even the homosexuals in Harlem, which is bursting with them, are brash, daring, cop-baiting individualists—when you're competing with other lean and hungry cats for the sirloins of life. After I was given a fishy eye because of my dress a number of times, my refuge in casual Village-type clothes underwent a change, and I dressed as rifle-hard and classy as I could when I later did my uptown balling.

What had happened inside me was this: I realized that downtown, in white society, especially the knowing, introspective, intellectual-literary kind, we put much value on "good looks" in the sense of paying excruciating attention to wart-tiny details of face and figure, and going into a tailspin when someone has facial one-upmanship over us. But up here in Harlem, where everyone is sunburned for life and can have little of that false self-love in what a blind fate has dealt them, good looks are *earned* by the way in which you bring art (dress, a cool mustache, the right earrings) to shine up an indifferent nature. The Negro has been and is an artist out of necessity not necessarily a fine artist but a human one; and if you want to score in Negro society you have to compete within the rules that an *original* kind of tough life has laid down. I wanted to score. The romantic-fantasizing me had lain flabbily undeveloped on its Villagey couch of yearning for too long, and I knew that if I wanted the chicks and the heart-deep kicks I had to get with it in a hurry.

I learned not only to dress, but to bargain with hustlers, keep my appetite in my pants and not show it, and develop all of the masculine wiles that I had once attributed to philistines with grudging acknowledgment of their effectiveness, but scorn as far as I was concerned. I became careful about money after I had been suckered out of perhaps $50, either by girls who promised two tricks and gave only one (or none) or "guides" who maintained they knew great flesh-parlors, and then disappeared over the squeezed-together Harlem roofs after letting me wait on a fourth-floor landing while they made the "arrangements." I was being shaped by the environment in which I was trying to make it, and while I never yielded up my total personality I cut out many of the affected, indecisive mannerisms that almost seem to be the norm in bookish white society.

Pleasure was my business in Harlem and I had to approach it like a business-man; I had to control my wandering kicks and appreciation to a technique for getting what I wanted. Along the way I picked up, almost without knowing it, 100 small bits of advice and know-how: never turn your back on a bar when standing there, it makes you conspicuous and is in bad taste; come on slowly and coolly with a hustling girl after looking them *all* over (Negro bar-buddies hammered this home), since you're a man and have the good money in your pocket or you wouldn't be there; ask for no favors, butt into *no* fights or arguments ("You might get hurt bad, Dick!"), show courtesy and good humor when put down by some h-high or drunken chick climbing a peak of meanness within herself; always buy a bouncer or bartender a drink when you can afford it; remember that music, sports and money are driving, magnetic topics in Harlem and will always get you an interesting conversation if you're hung up or ill at ease.

I had come uptown with a predisposition. Not only did I love the girls and the music—which reflected each other in warmth, drive, flashing humor, lusty beat—but my eye and heart had always been a pushover for the stylish, spirited Negro ace as well. It was therefore no strain on my grimly introspective makeup (a complaint I heard from several other isolated white writers who were drawn to

Harlem but felt hurtingly awkward when they tried it) to make my way into colored society, to dig the tasty food, kibitz easily in the luncheonettes, listen to the finest and hippest jukeboxes for hours and be a happy addict with my quarters. I felt I was being educated and given a human feast at the same time; nor did I prey on it. I gave both spirit and gold and the greatest appreciation for what I got, and can say now, without self-consciousness, that the human exchange was equal. Most of the Caucasian men who come to Harlem to get laid are looking for easy eats, and carry their stiff marriage of caution and superiority so squarely that they are verbally speared in a dozen ways without knowing it. All they hear is laughter and they wonder why. The other greys who come, including myself, are the imaginative, sensitive, troubled, daring kicks-seekers who the hipper local Negroes take to without any break in stride, recognizing masculine brothers in the eternal war with fate, chicks and George Washington's dollar. There was no segregation once I got in. The masculine brother idea, like the female sister one, is a reality in Harlem, not just words; broke and drunk I found no trouble or shame in borrowing money for carfare back to the Village, which I repaid the following week, or even getting my ashes hauled on credit (which is difficult and embarrassing to set up with the average, where's-my-next-movie-money-coming-from hustler, unless she digs you in the boy-girl-moonlight sense.)

But I also saw by about my third month in Harlem the low, cruel, ignorant, selfish, small-minded side of uptown life. I was first cheated out of money by lies and juicy come-ons which never matured. O.K., one expects to be played for a sucker in the tenderloin unless one keeps one's wits, and I learned what every pilgrim through the thighs and breasts of Fleshville and Champagne Corners has had drilled into his bank account since man first sought pleasure. I accepted it. But my finer senses, if after all this I can legitimately use the phrase, were humbled time and again by the sight of men beating women, hustlers drunkenly cursing and clawing each other, friends of mine (Negro men and women both) boasting of how they had cheated ConEd out of money by fixing the meter or how they had boosted goods from Macy's and Bloomingdale's, or how some date I was out with was afraid to go home to her old man (the pimp she lived with) because he'd take three-quarters of what I gave her and beat the living jazz out of her if she held out. (This particular girl once hid in my apartment for three days out of fear, narcotizing herself, among other ways, with watching Darrin McGavin as Mike Hammer on TV and impatiently waiting for Darrin to "get to that dirty fighting man, cause it's *too* much!")

I saw the most fantastic lying—not the exception, but the rule, with the gang I travelled with—to get money for h (heroin), jewelry, clothes, whiskey, pot, the latest Big Maybelle record, money out of a sucker, stranger, relative, brother, mother: it made no difference. Yet side-by-side with this I saw the human good that lay just an inch away from its flip into unarguable nastiness. For example the great naturalness and wit of most of the people I got to know—their fluid ease, generosity, life-shrewdness, laughing philosophical fatalism— when taken a notch to the left became recklessness, hostility without restraint, the pettiest haggling over coin, the most sullen selfishness. The qualities I dug in Harlem night-time Negroes often became, in other words, viciousness I repudiated in all human beings who were bent on degradation of another, violence, who whined, fibbed, stole, backed out of jams, played others for fall-guys, the gold in their teeth and back pocket. Apart from my jazz and sex self-interest—my plain thirst—I came to Harlem with an open mind that was ready and willing to find beauty in much that the squares, or engineers as we called them, backed away from. I found that I, too, backed like a trooper. I should have realized that I couldn't get my kicks, my needs fulfilled, without a corresponding loss on the other side of the human balance sheet. *Was it then people like myself who helped degrade the Negro by coming to his community in order to cut myself a piece of the pleasure pie? Was it my needs of ear and flesh that helped make some of the colored whores themselves, and understandably cheat and con on the side, because they knew why I was there and laughed up their mutual sleeve at my so-called decent ethical standards?*

These were rough thoughts and I had to try and face them. I came to the conclusion that we fed each other, the Harlem night-time Negro and myself, but that the revulsion and often amazement I felt at the lying and cheating couldn't be my responsibility because, what the hell, I wasn't God. It went on when I and no white spy was present, in this Lenox Avenue hot-box, not because of any Gene Talmadge bullshit about colored inferiority but because the people were dollar-hungry, haphazardly educated, often ignorant (hardly stupid—I've got the scabs of many a mental thrust!), street-arab tough, and ruthlessly indifferent or *foreign* to middle-class morality. They lived by night, in the old movie title, and they hustled their bucks and jollies any way they could; they had lied, spat, fisted, grabbed their way up from five in a room, rats, bugs, the unflushable toilet and the leaking ceiling, the misery-drowning bottle and the magic needle, mama doing the two-backed bit to make the rent and new-compact money ("I'm the third generation of prostitutes," a business-like Negro mother told me with flat dignity) and their attitude towards getting what they wanted was the hardest, most selfish, screw-the-ethics approach I had ever been up against.

3

I was hypnotized by it for a while—the way the sheltered sissy-rich kid in movies always is by brushes with the underworld—but after a year of hitting Harlem three or four time a week, day and night, the fascination wore itself down and hardened into skepticism and suspicion. My heart no longer winced at the sights of misery and humiliation that I saw on the streets; I looked for the further truth, behind the too-glib appeal to my humanity, where before I accepted hard-luck stories on their running-sore face value. (As James Baldwin and Richard Wright have both pointed out, the Negro's suffering has been so full that it's often hard for him to refrain from using it, actor-style, to make it pay off. And who's to blame him from the distance of this printed page—while, similarly, who wants to be suckered and played the jerk close up?) I got to know, by my uptown education, something of what it's like to be an average Negro in any of the big-city ghettoes, how you harden your heart, your jaw, your stomach, take what you can get away with, spit at fate, laugh at wounds, conceivably dance at funerals to keep your own spirits alive. I appreciated the life-induced toughness of the hustlers I knew, by the dozen, even while their callousness and ignorance never failed to scrape against my upbringing like sandpaper. They had begun life, before American society had been wrenched open to make way for the man of color, as the very social garbage of U.S. existence; and if they didn't nastily laugh or scornfully sway with the right-is-white whip the very humanity in them would have said nix, nix, this can't be, and they would have used razor or gas to find pride's haven. And I, also a poor up-against-it mortal (but in a different way) had once, too, been ripe for the big sleep when my hope of happiness had fled, and here I was trading on the dirty pleasure streets with these my sisters and brethren in hardship!

Even after I had lost my girlish, milky notions about the natural greatness of Negroes—a defiant liberalism and sense of identification stemming in part from my being the unreligious modern American Jew who feels only the self-pitying sting of his identity without the faith—I was still haunted by Harlem. True, irony and a slitted eye had replaced to some extent my former urge to dig all the sights and sounds. I was more realistic, cynical, harder and even nastier on occasion with the hustling girls than I would ever have dreamed I could be when I first entered paradise. I would no longer allow myself to be taken for quarters or drinks by one-armed and one-eyed beggars and bar-jockeys (who were actually less handicapped with the facts of life than yours truly). The promise of a wild blow-job by some outwardly gorgeous mulatto chick was now tempered by experience, by the coldness that could freeze the bed once the money had been paid, the quickness, indifference, cop-out; I could no longer sweepingly arc my dreams of sex and desire on to a Harlem that I had gotten to know from the spare-ribs up. I was more like Sam Spade now than Stephen Dedalus, or his crude U.S. equivalent. But even so, I still got a special boot out of walking the streets of Harlem, of mingling in its life to the depth I did (which went beyond the whore and bar-type acquaintanceships to two fairly solid friendships with working-class Negroes) that I never received downtown in white society.

This next is an uncomfortable point to write about: but it's true that when I strode the Harlem avenues I not only had an absence of the physical fear my buddies tell me they feel above 110th St., I had a sense of *security* and well-being precisely because of my color. For the first time in my adult life I felt completely confident and masterful in my relationship to both sexes because society judged me the superior, just as in a different, Irish-bar type scene it made me stand out unto myself because of the Yiddish bit. In others words, I was the human worm turning; even more true and paradoxical is the fact that I was a better, more capable, objective and gentlemanly person among Negroes (for the one big reason that my security could never be threatened) than I was among whites. So oddly enough my Harlem experiences made me feel both how and why many uptown Negroes act as they do and also made me feel like a southern white, understanding for the first time the tremendous psychological *impregnability* to the cracker (every white man has a built-in colonel-kit!) in having an "inferior" class beneath him. It was an astonishing

revelation to realize that you could be a better person—more attentive, calmer, happier, and that last word is the truth—for the *wrong
reasons,* that is by realizing that the people in Harlem wanted you
to like them, and that if they permitted themselves any expression
of hatred it was clear that it was an aspect of themselves they were
crying out against rather than you.

I am not proud to write this: but it's true, or was in my case,
and since I like you am wantonly and unmitigatedly human, I took
advantage of this psychological reality to give myself the basic happiness I wanted. It brought out my best as a person among other
people, and yet it's likely that my very security helped reinforce the
insecurity of many of the Negroes I knew towards whites! (Thus
does one human being use another for reasons that are deeper than
morality—because of our inconsolable life-needs as individuals.) I
was the predatory male in Harlem, which means the true male, re-
fined, amiable, sure-footed and sure-minded because I knew that fulfillment of my needs (not downtown blockage and anxiety) was
right around the corner whenever I wanted it. In the village I always
felt, like most of us, that I was in equal competition so intense that it
brought out my worst and made me want to withdraw rather then
come out in all my potential manhood and therefore complete humanity. I can only justify this Harlem-using by my needs as a human
being, and if I didn't know how desperate the necessitities of life can
be—to the point where the impossibly jammed-up contemporary person must hunt in every offbeat street and alley that the mind can
conceive to assuage them—I would feel more guilt than my picture
of total justice says is right.

4

It is unrealistic to think the same attitude holds in Harlem that
exists downtown in the Village, or in midtown, or any of the new
mixed housing projects, where Negroes are increasingly your neighbors, friends, lovers, wife, husband, landlord—Christ, your goddamn
analyst! Harlem is Harlem, the brutal, frantic, special scene of the
big-city Negro in America until this time, and the white-black contrast still maintains its unique, soon-to-be-blended (as Negroes increasingly crash out) charge for the pioneering ofay who crosses
the line with nerve-ends humming. You are entering Negro America,
man, and you carry with you—despite your personal courage or lack

of it—an unspoken message stamped on your skin, Jim! You are there for a reason, as are the second-rate white dentists, real-estate finaglers, jewelers, optometrists, pawn-brokers, and so are the colored, because until recently they were hemmed in as neatly as an enemy. Why dodge the sociological exoticism in your being there? But why, also, dodge the needs that led you there? If you love music, beat, chicks, color, barbecue, wild inventive humor with the stab of truth in it— why shouldn't you be there when your own life has denied you these things? But, hungup human that you are, you can never mate the pleasure of Harlem with the pain; your mind doesn't want to see that the kicks you love breed in a white-ringed pesthole (I exclude the secret few upper middle-class hideaways) whose stink offends your very soul, like an unaired bathroom. I could never immunize myself (nor should I have!) to the garbage in the streets, the obsessive ads and shops for hair-straightening and beauty treatments (not so un-like my own nose-bobbing, is it, in the attempt to gleam like a clean-cut White Protestant beauty?), the pawnshops five to a block, the rat-infested tenements, the thousands of dollars spent on TV's and radio-phonographs at the sacrifice of medical aid and sanitation, the feverish traffic in drugs, the hordes of sullen-faced, corner-haunting hustlers, the waste of money on adolescent trinkets, the wild red rage on the broken-beerbottle 5 A.M. streets and the ceaseless stealing (how many times have I had my change stolen from bar and lunch-counter while I was feeding the juke and trusting my night-time friends!) And yet, my conscience sneers to me now as I write this, what did you expect, what could you have rightly expected—a heaven of sensuality without the pissmire of sociology?

I sincerely doubt that even God could marry the discrepancies: namely, the boots and joys of Harlem life for soul- as well as penis-starved human beings like myself, who could get the needed equiva-lent *nowhere* else in this greatest city on the globe, along with its ugliness, .45 calibre toughness, and kick-him-when-he's-just-getting-up attitude (not when he's down—that's too easy). The life-scarred pave-ment that reaches from 110th and Lenox to 155th breeds the one intergrown with the other. And yet if you look at Harlem without any attempt at morality at all, from a strictly physical and blindly sensuous point of view, it is the richest kind of life one can ever see in American action as far as the fundamental staples of love, hate, joy, sorrow, street-poetry, dance and death go. The body and texture of its solid reality is a 100 times stronger, sharper to the nostrils, eye, ear, heart, than what we downtown greys are used to. And within a decade (some say two) it will probably end as Negroes become increasingly integrated and sinewed into the society around them. I will truly hate to see Harlem go—where will *I* seek then in my time of need, O merciless life?—and yet I would obviously help light the match that blows it out of existence.

At a buzzing bar I used to go to on Lenox between 110th and 115th Streets, where the bait paraded boldly, drunkenly, or screw-you-Jack around the circular wood, wanting your wallet but trying to size you up as a plainclothes cop or not, the makers of Hennesey Whiskey had put up a sign which I'm sure was designed for the neighborhood trade all over Harlem. It said: "Ask For A White Cadillac." This bizarre drink was just good old Hennesey along with milk, mixed together in a high-ball glass. But the name, the music and color and swing of the image, was a laughing ball to these pleasure-bored sports and duchesses, who were belting White Cadillacs (and perhaps the cat next to me was an off-duty chauffeur) at 3 A.M. while the rocking box dealt out sounds like hip bullets, and the entire bar shrank into a black-and-tan fantasy of booze, wailing laughter, the crack of palm on face, tears, the bargain of bucks for ass, and the lusty, caressing accents of, "You can take your motherf—king drink and stick it in your motherf—king ear, darling!"

So long, dark dream mistress of my adolescence and educator of my so-called manhood!

S. P. Lomax

now living in Amsterdam, Holland, has published widely in the Danish and Dutch press. Before leaving New York almost five years ago, he was published in *Artesian* and other little magazines. Currently he is writing educational material for *Actuele Onderwerpen Reeks* and completing a novel, *Conny,* soon to be published in Holland.

Pollution

"WHAT WAS that supposed to mean, Harry? Now what was that supposed to mean? And you're always so cool, man. Like I told you, all you have to do is wait and it'll come."

"I don't know what you're getting at. All I said was . . ."

"I know what you said."

"But . . ."

"Forget it, man. Just forget it." The Chevy moved through the twilight streets, turning swiftly onto Third Avenue, and sped downtown. Harry peered to the left, recording the streets as he drove. He had never expected Cecil to be that sensitive. He thought he could swing more freely with him. "But man, you got to tell me just what it was that . . ."

"I don't have to tell you nothing, dig? Nothing. If you want to hear sounds tonight, cool. If not, that's good too." It's my fault, reflected Cecil. I should never have let him get that far. Give them an inch, not even an inch, and . . . But I thought he was different. Why should I have thought that? Maybe I wanted to. Maybe I needed to. Maybe anything. Man, we are sick. Paranoiac. But why are we? That's the question. That is *the* question. *And you know what? The chick's not even a little earthy. I don't see what Bela sees in her. Man, she comes on just like a white chick. Not even a little earthy.*

"Almost missed it."

"Who's blowing?"

"Some new cat, I think he's from Tennessee or somewhere. You down?"

"Yeah."

"All right then." Harry pulled up to the parking meter. They took off their overcoats and dropped them in the back seat. Cecil stepped out of the car without his customary briskness for the shadow of melancholia had fallen over him. He felt remote, uninvolved. He would probably feel that way for a time. Why hadn't he grown used to it? Had anyone? Could anyone? "Table?" the hawknosed, phthisic waiter asked. "No, man," he replied, scanning the bar for space. The baritone sax rocked soulfully, voluptuously. The musician swayed to his own swinging rhythms. "Wailing, huh?" Harry asked, popping his fingers. He was always a bit off the beat and in a vague way this always irritated Cecil. "Yeah, wailing. That the cat?"

"No, he blows trombone." They sat at the bar, faced the bandstand. They sat bemused, rapt throughout the extended solo, absorbing the involuted and gutty tones. Behind the dark glasses, the player yearned, searched. Something welled up gratifyingly within Cecil; a sudden flash of pride. He knew that as much as he might try, Harry could not quite make the liaison with the music necessary for total enjoyment. This, at least, was a place they could not go, not really. They tried though. And how they tried! He was glad that this was something wholly Negro, that had remained essentially inviolate despite their concerted effort to bastardize it. Everything they touched, reflected Cecil, they contaminated, dirtied. Even those like Harry, Harry who put in a sincere attempt to learn, to know, to be a part of. There was no touching point. The wall was there. And the wall was impenetrable. "Blowing his chops off, heh Cec?"

"I mean."

"Wish Cassie was here."

"Thought she was coming."

"Naw, got to work late."

"A drag." Guess Cassie's all right for him, Cecil thought. She doesn't act like a white chick. That makes him dig her I suppose. He wanted a black chick who acted black, whatever that's supposed to mean. Makes him feel whiter, makes him feel pure fay boy. Don't worry, dad, you're pure fay boy all right. Nothing'll ever change that. You're fay from your chittlins on out. . . . The pianist struck a plangent chord à la Bud Powell; the drummer rolled to a thump. The number was over. Intermittent applause. Sipping beer, Cecil peered through the room's half-light, looking for familiar faces. None. A long-necked white girl with limp sandy hair leaned languorously on her boy friend's shoulder. She played idly with the olive at the bottom of the martini. Her boy friend closed his eyes as though he were drinking in the club's atmosphere. Noise. Eyes moving quickly in sudden surreptitious glances around the room. Posturing, elegant and affected. The jazz scene. Everything they put their hands on . . . everything. Cecil subdued his upbubbling bitterness. He was there to enjoy the music, not to criticize, analyze. Perhaps he would break the tension. Talk about something else. "How's the trip coming?"

"Fine, man," Harry grinned. His up-drawn shoulders relaxed noticeably.

He was glad that it had only been a passing thing. Cecil meant quite a lot to him as a friend and the fact that the race thing had to get in the way, even occasionally, annoyed him. Between sets, they turned towards each other, beer glasses cold at the end of exploring fingers, talking about the trip. Harry had decided to go out and look the landscape over; he wasn't sure as things stood whether he really wanted to live there or not, but a doctor friend of his told him that things were great: weather, jobs, entertainment, women. It was always the same with them, Cecil reflected. No matter how homely, corny, or just plain ineffectual they were they could always move easily in the world. Chicks were forever available for them—his women as well as their own. The jobs, the babes, the happiness, the land. *The land of the fay.* It was big and various for them; it was comfortable and uninvolved. But wherever he would go there would be a whole network of tradition going against him. Through the sound haze he could hear Harry's voice droning seriously on, "And then, of course, there's the matter of getting set up with some fine thing, you know."

"Hip."

"You see, it'll be all a wasteland if it's just a matter of working and cooling. There just must be that fine thing."

"What about Cassie?" Harry was not prepared for the question. He had considered Cecil a bit too sophisticated for such a question.

"Well, man," he began nervously, "I did do some thinking about it and . . ."

Cecil could tell that he was lying. Their eyes met for an instant, darted away. "Yeah, man, I understand." He spun forward from the bar, obliquely; watched the alternate combo take the stand. "Well, I was going to bring it up with her like soon," Harry went on. "But you know how she feels about the coast."

"Yeah, I know." In an off sense, Cecil was enjoying Harry's uneasiness, but the bare lying bugged him. Why couldn't Harry just say that he didn't intend to tell her and leave it at that? Why couldn't he just say that she was one of those "over-there" people and that she didn't count? It would have been much simpler and he would have understood. Why dodge and swerve and b.s.? It wasn't necessary or didn't he know that? The voice droned on. Passively, he allowed himself to be convinced, feigning full acceptance of the lie. The quaver in

Harry's voice unnerved him and he cut it short. "I think they're ready to blow."

"Yeah." The group was too loud, their only grace being that they blew with conviction and authentic funk. Harry seemed agitated by Cecil's brusqueness. From time to time, he peered over his shoulder at him, then looked quickly, uneasily away. He frowned, pursuing private thoughts in silence. From the left Bela and his new find entered. She was tall, well-tuned. She walked ahead of him, swiftly, gracefully, smiling nervously. Heads turned, dug with ogling, incredulous eyes. Cecil caught himself ogling too. Why, he mused, did it always happen that way? Attractive colored babe hooked up with a raggedy paddy. What was that supposed to make her? They approached the men at the bar. Bela spoke first: "Harry you know already. Cecil, this is Seraphita." She smiled an indifferent smile.

"Pleased to meet you," Cecil said hoarsely.

"Hi," Seraphita breathed. Her flesh exuded a keen sweet smell. "How about let's gettin' a table?" Bela suggested. The four of them moved to a table in the corner near the wall where the light was less pronounced. Bela ordered the drinks and began monopolizing the conversation. He had just finished putting over some deal. He had just returned from Paris as Macy's chief bra buyer. His bleating voice whined on, riding annoyingly above the music. Cecil continued to stare unwittingly. "Bud's over there now, you know. Wailing his natural chops off. Caught him six nights straight. I think after this deal I'm in for a substantial raise. Moving upper and upper. Say, looks like I'm doing all the talking. So what's been happening back here in Never-Never Land."

"Aw, man, like you ain't been gone that long. Stop the jive," Harry asserted. Seraphita smiled coyly, her eyes riveted on Bela's mouth. She absorbed his every word. "You from New York?" Cecil asked.

"No," she responded curtly as though it were an effort to talk.

"Been here long?"

"Not very." And with an exquisite hand gesture, she wordlessly let him know that the questions annoyed her. Cecil drank his bourbon down in a shot. Hinkty, he thought. What she wants is what she's got and that lets me out. She sure has made the move. Anything but a nigger is what she wants to be. He felt the rage come up full into his throat—rage and helplessness. "So how's it been with you, Cec?" He was an instant too slow in answering, his thoughts had taken a morbid turn. "Nothing, Bela. Still struggling with the books. Still trying hard to make it. Can't see the light yet."

"You'll make it, man. You got the stuff."

"Yeah, sure."

"Cecil's not in too good a mood tonight," Harry offered.

"No? What's the matter, man?"

"Let him tell you," Cecil said, pointing angrily to Harry. "He brought it up." A thrill of tension drifted amidst the four. Seraphita sipped her drink slowly. Harry sat with a quizzical and reflective smile, studying his fingers. Bela smiled weakly. Cecil stared vacantly in the direction of the bandstand. They were always putting words in your mouth. If I didn't feel good, I would have said so. He sat hunched over his empty glass, feeling alone. "Now why don't you be a nice boy and apologize?" Seraphita said, placing a smooth, well-cared-for hand on his forearm.

"For what? Apologize for what?" he snapped.

"For being a party pooper. Everything was going nicely until you got evil." He breathed in deeply, holding in the strain. What was she trying to prove? Nervously, he rubbed his forehead. He saw the subtle smiles on the two white faces. He told himself he would not blow up. That's what they were waiting for, he thought. They probably saw that he liked her and that only made his attempt at control that much more difficult. Her hand still rested calmly on his arm. She smiled her lovely smile; he felt himself undone. The subtle sorcery of her face was nothing short of hypnotic. The more he looked at her, the more he detested Bela. "Sorry, fellows," he said in a near whisper.

"Apology accepted," Bela announced.

"See how much nicer it is when you're nice?" She was still smiling. Cecil nodded. He felt foolish but he was not certain why. Bela went back to talking shop and Seraphita went back to drinking in his every word. The waiter returned and they reordered. Cecil drank his second drink and watched her out of the corner of his eye. She was inexpressibly beautiful: liquid eyes; slim, shapely body; splendid poise. He sat mute and motionless, digging everything. She did not once turn his way. Eyes only for Bela. A feeling of profound alienation came over him. He didn't belong there with Harry and Bela and her. They made a trio, their own kind of trio. The invisible wall urged itself up, higher, higher. It was as though it were their party and he an encroacher, out of it. He strained to block out their presence, steeping himself in the music. The question recurred in his mind ringing resonantly: Why him? Why Bela? Why any white guy for that matter? Then the all too bald truth of it rushed in on him. It was painful, unwieldy truth, one that he wanted to rip out of his mind. Suddenly he was sad with a sense of heaviness and inadequacy. He stood up. "Where you going?" Harry asked.

"Got to go."

"Aw, come on, Cec. The evening's just started. I thought we'd catch a couple more sets and . . ."

"Later," he insisted and moved away from the table. "Glad to have met you, Seraphita," he mumbled. She fluttered her fingers for a goodby. He could feel their eyes on him as he pushed through the door.

The black, light-reflecting water slushed sibilantly against the river wall. He sat with his fists plunged deeply, tightly in his pants pockets, legs extended. A dull, indistinct ache numbed his chest. Along the promenade the couples walked huddling intimately, murmuring low, an occasional explosive giggle joined the water's lapping among the night sounds. The strange sombre lustrous beauty of the river dulled his vision and he thought of his room with the masses of books. Bloodless books. Lifeless books. He thought of the long and painful way he had come and of the long and painful way that was left. It was too much, too much. The meaningless monotonous circle his life had become. He pushed up from the bench and walked along the park path that led to the overpass. He could feel the couples in the dark making love, feel their caresses, their rising ardors. As he came to the end of the path he saw one couple at the corner of the apron of light. Involuntarily, he stood rapt in absolute muse watching them. The boy impelled the male import to its utmost with a kind of madness, the girl retorted in kind, spurring on the male will, the complete affirmation of blunt, formidable will. Snapping out of his reverie, feeling ashamed for having seen them, he rushed on, dashing up the stairs, traversing the overpass. His body shuddered as he ran. Tears suffused his eyes. He felt the spot on his arm where a soft and easy weight had lain earlier in the evening. "Everything they touch," he said, rage choking his tones to a whisper. "Everything!"

Dennis Lynds

now living in Santa Barbara, has published poetry and short stories in an amazing number of magazines and reviews, as well as publishing two novels, *Combat Soldier* and *Uptown Downtown*. In 1956 one of his stories was selected for the Martha Foley *Best Short Stories* collection. Born in St. Louis, Mr. Lynds has lived in New York since 1933, with time out for sojourns in Denver, Syracuse, London, Paris and parts of Texas.

A night in Syracuse

HE STOOD just off the concrete at the side of the highway, his weight on his good leg. The last light of the sun was over Buffalo behind him. A smell of cooking hung in the air. The low frame houses and factory yards were orange in the fading sunlight. Men in shirtsleeves sat on the open porches. Inside the houses the women rattled dishes, chattered, their high voices floating across the highway with the smell of cooking. The men on the porches watched him idly as he stood waiting for a ride. Their minds were busy with their own problems. They waited for the call to dinner.

When the new red Oldsmobile passed he did not flag it. New cars did not stop. New cars drove past as if the drivers could not see him. Women, local businessmen, and new cars never stopped. This time he was wrong. The new Oldsmobile skidded to a halt fifty feet past him. He picked up his suitcase and limped up the road to the red car. The driver, a small, fat man, drove off the instant the door was closed. The new car had bucket seats and a stick shift. The fat man shifted hard into high.

"Almost missed you," the driver said. "You forget to thumb?"

"New car," he said.

"People are bastards," the driver said. "I'm a salesman, shoes. How far you going?"

"New York."

"I turn off at Syracuse," the driver said. "Must be hard on you hitching. I mean, with the leg."

"When do we get to Syracuse?"

"Before midnight, I fly low," the driver said. "This baby can take it. What happened? Polio?"

"I was run down by a chariot on the high seas."

"Okay, I mind my own business," the driver said.

The driver took out a cigarette and lighted it. Annoyed, the driver smoked and watched the highway ahead that was purple in the twilight. He paid no attention to the driver. He was used to the annoyance they showed when he would not talk about his leg. A hazard of the road. They wanted to know how it felt to be a cripple.

They wanted to know what a cripple thought about. It fascinated them. To talk about his leg seemed to make them feel better. They were all talkers. That was why they picked him up. The leg was a bonus, and when he would not talk about the leg it stopped them for a time. It did not stop this one for long as the dark road stretched ahead.

"Relatives in New York?"

"No," he said.

"A job?"

"I'll probably get a job," he said.

"Footloose and fancy-free," the driver said. "How old are you? Twenty-three? Twenty-four?"

"Twenty-six," he said. "I'm twenty-six years old, I've been crippled since I was five, I've been to college, I like to hitch-hike, I work in print shops, I'm visiting New York because I've never been to New York, I expect I'll work in a print shop in New York."

"Too big for me, New York," the driver said.

"I like big cities," he said.

He made his voice become pleasant. Anger did no good. Most of them, like the fat man, did not hear the anger but only the information, the conversation they wanted from him.

"No one knows you, or looks at you, or gives a damn," the driver said. "Give me a small town, a small city. Syracuse, now that ain't a bad town. They know me in Syracuse. One time I was selling. . . ."

He rested his head against the back of the seat, his eyes half closed and staring ahead. The driver talked. He had learned how to answer just enough to keep the driver happy without actually saying anything or really listening. He rested his head and watched the lighted towns and solitary farmhouses as the Oldsmobile drove on in the night. At night, in a moving car, one town was just like another. They could have been anywhere. First there were the lighted windows of the outskirts. Then the quick blaze of main street, the red and blue neon of the taverns, the bright marquees of the movie houses, the people, the girls in their swinging dresses. The trees again, and the solitary lighted windows, and once more the dark highway with the distant lights of farmhouses. He could be anywhere. New York, or Wyoming, or Alabama, or, maybe, even some town in Siberia. A long, dark highway between fields and trees and hills, with the sudden lights of passing cars and the far-off lights of the farmhouses. Then more outskirts, and neon taverns, and people, and outskirts, and the highway a solid black beyond the beams of the head-lights.

"This side or the other side?"

The driver spoke in a loud, sullen voice. The driver, surly, almost angry, because he had been asleep in the deep bucket seat of the new car. His neck was stiff, his good leg numb. He sat up to look at the lights of Syracuse.

"I can let you out here or take you through," the driver said. "I turn off the other side."

"I'll go through," he said. "Thanks."

On the far side of the city the driver let him out at a corner near a tavern. The red car drove off. He rested his suitcase beside the highway. The tavern back along the road had blue and yellow neon signs. It was a low frame building surrounded by dark apart-ment houses tall in the night. There was a sidewalk that seemed to end on either side of the tavern as if built only for the tavern. He picked up his suitcase and limped toward the tavern. He went inside and walked through the noise and smoke to the bar. Before the bar-tender came to take his order, he saw the woman.

She was not that beautiful. She probably had been once, but there were wrinkles around her eyes and on her throat. Her long brown hands were rough. She was solid where once she must have been slender, hard where once she had been soft. He saw all that, and she was still more than beautiful. Her breasts were high and her skin smooth. Like a statue in brown marble. The darkness of her skin made her eyes brighter. She had green eyes. He saw that even through the smoke. Her nose was small and straight, the nostrils lightly flared. An oval face and long brown hair tied back with a green ribbon. She wore a green dress. The dress had no shoulders to cover the smooth brown of her skin. She was not a young woman, and she sat alone at a table near the bar.

"Just sightseein'?" the bartender said to him.

"Beer," he said.

"Only bottles."

"A bottle," he said.

She was drinking beer. Her hand moved on her glass as if feeling its texture, caressing. He imagined the touch of her long fingers on his face. She did not notice him. Her eyes were looking toward a section of the bar where a small man stood alone. The small man had his back to her. The man had a lined face, grey, and he was drinking straight whisky. Every second some part of the small man moved. His hands touched his thin face. His tongue licked his lips. His fingers tapped on the bar. He moved his feet up and down from the bar rail. His eyes flickered around the faces in the tavern. He smiled and scowled. His fingers worked through his grey hair. His face bent toward his whisky glass as he drank. Once the small man looked toward him and the small man's eyes were like the thin ice on a mud puddle at the side of a road on a cold morning. The small man drank steadily. He, himself, drank three bottles of beer and watched the woman for over a half an hour before he picked up his beer and took it with him as he limped to her table.

"I'm passing through," he said. "To New York. I don't know anyone here."

"That's too bad," the woman said.

She had a low voice, soft, and yet a little hoarse, not young. A low, hoarse, and yet steady voice without any particular inflection or accent. Her green eyes barely looked up at him.

"Can I buy you something?" he said.

"You don't know me, boy."

"I'd like to," he said. "Maybe a beer?"

"New York," she said. "I used to live in New York. A while ago."

"I've never been there," he said.

"You want to buy me a beer, boy?"

"Maybe sit and talk," he said.

"You buy me a beer then," the woman said.

He sat down facing her. After the waiter had come and gone, she drank her beer and moved her long fingers up and down on her glass. She neither spoke nor looked at him. Close to her she was, in a way, even more beautiful. The wrinkles at her throat and around her eyes muted in the dim light now that he sat close and on the same level. Her brown skin not hard but only smooth all the way down from her neck to the swell of her breasts that rose smoothly up from the cloth of the green dress. Her hands, rough on the glass, moved gently and with a slow grace. An ease about her, here close and facing her.

"Do you always drink beer?" he said.

"Just driving through?" she said.

"Hitch-hiking," he said. "I never owned a car, never had the money. I never wanted to own a car. If you own things they can hold you."

"Everyone owns something," the woman said.

"You see things hitch-hiking," he said. "I've seen most of the country."

"That's good," she said

"My uncle owns a farm, up in Wisconsin," he said. "I lived there for ten years with him and my cousins. Four boys. With four of them, and this leg of mine, I didn't have to work much. I carried food out to them and worked with the chickens. I know all about chickens. When I was old enough I got out of there."

"You didn't like chickens?" the woman said.

"You can learn on a farm, though," he said. "I saw a fish hawk, an osprey, tangle with an eagle. The osprey was fishing in the river. It got a fish and started off with it. This damned big eagle came out of nowhere. An eagle can't begin to fly as good as an osprey, only the osprey was carrying that fish. As long as the osprey carried the fish it couldn't get away from the eagle. So it dropped the fish. Without the fish it flew rings around the eagle. The eagle didn't give a damn, all it wanted was that fish. It got the fish before the fish hit the ground. All the damned osprey could do was fly around and scream. The eagle didn't even look back."

"You don't like eagles," the woman said.

"I hate eagles," he said.

"What do you do about it?" the woman said.

"On the farm I used to carry a .22 rifle and shoot at them," he said. "I think it's illegal, but I never hit one anyway."

"You tried to hit an eagle with a .22 rifle?" the woman said. "You are an optimist, boy."

"I guess I am," he said. Her green eyes were looking somewhere over his shoulder. "I saw you when I came in."

"Why did you go to that farm?" she said.

"I saw you sitting here alone," he said.

"You hated that farm," she said.

"My mother died," he said. "My father died a long time ago. My mother had cancer. You couldn't tell, she was always so pretty."

"It shows at the end," the woman said.

She had not really looked at him since he had taken the seat facing her. She talked to him, and drank the beer, and once or twice her eyes had turned in his direction, but she had not really looked at him. She looked at her beer glass as she moved her hands on it, and she looked at nothing, the green eyes flat and unfocused and looking at space, and she looked at the back of the small man at the bar. The small man drank one whisky after another. He did not look behind him. Nor had she smiled once.

"In the beginning nothing shows," the woman said.

"Is Syracuse your home? I mean, your hometown?"

"Philadelphia."

"I was born in Minneapolis," he said, "but we moved to Chicago. They had better clinics in Chicago."

"Chicago's a big city," the woman said.

"Did you go to college in Philadelphia?"

"College?" the woman said.

"I went for two years," he said. "My uncle thought it would be nice to have an accountant in the family. I did good in the wrong things. I liked the wrong things. History, literature, political science. It made him mad. So I left."

"Temple University," the woman said. "I went to dances. I went to a lot of dances with a lot of boys. I was very popular. That's important to a girl, very important."

"You're beautiful," he said.

The green eyes, unsmiling, glanced toward him, flicked across his face, and then looked away toward the small man or at nothing, he could not tell.

"Don't you have anything better to do, boy?"

"No," he said.

"All right," she said, "then buy me another beer."

He waved to the waiter. The waiter came and he ordered two more beers.

"I don't have to go to New York tonight," he said.

The waiter placed the beer bottles on the table. Both bottles were wet with white foam. The waiter took his money and left. The woman poured her beer.

"You mean we could go someplace tonight?" the woman said.

"I'd like that," he said.

She nodded. She still did not smile or look at him, but she nodded now. The nod was neither yes nor no, but only that she understood that he would like to go somewhere with her. Her eyes looked away toward the bar again. The nod of understanding became a nod of direction. He turned to look where she wanted him to look. The small man at the bar was having difficulty placing his empty glass back onto the bar. The glass struck the bar hard, loud.

The small man's head had begun to move back and forth as if loose on his thick neck, the grey head moving like the head of a hound sniffing the air for a scent.

"You'd never guess that he was handsome once, would you?" the woman said. "He was graduating from Law School and I was just a junior. Handsome, and nice, and very bright. It made me weak just to dance with him. It's not so bad when he's sober. Twenty years we've been married. This is his home, up here. He stokes boilers for General Electric at night. His father owned a factory here, but his father died and the family paid us off. Money goes fast with a drunk. You ever know how fast money can go with a drunk, boy?"

"You were alone," he said.

"I suppose I was," the woman said.

"I've got some money," he said.

"Good for you."

"Do you just wait for him?"

"I'm waiting," the woman said.

"He doesn't know you're here," he said.

"He knows, boy."

"So you wait for him?"

"Not much longer," the woman said. "Soon now."

"I've got enough money to go someplace," he said.

"A room?" the woman said. "The nigger girl and the cripple?"

"I saw you, you were alone, I didn't know."

"Didn't you, boy?" the woman said.

Now she looked at him, really looked. Her green eyes stared straight into his face, and her pale lips moved, opened, as if she were about to speak again. He waited, but she did not speak. Her pale lips still parted, she looked away. The small man at the bar had moved. The small man had turned. His thin hands lowered his whisky glass to the bar, misjudged the distance again, and the glass struck the bar hard and loud again, and the small man turned. The small man leaned with his back against the bar, his head moving back and forth as if searching the smoky air. The eyes that were like thin, dark water blinked and tried to focus. The small man smiled. His mouth was wet and his tongue licked out against his lips. The small man's lips moved, talked without a sound. He waved one thin hand before his eyes as if brushing away a mist. He took a slow breath. And his mouth opened wide.

"I HATE NIGGERS!!"

At first, as the shout echoed, the people in the tavern became silent, motionless as if frozen. The small man grinned and leaned with his back against the bar. Only the shout seemed to move in the silent tavern. The small man licked his lips, grinned, seemed to listen to the echo of his own sudden shout. The small man heard his own words, nodded up and down, listened and agreed, approved. The people in the tavern began to laugh. They moved, laughed, craned their necks to look through the smoke at the small man. The mouth of the bartender was annoyed, but his eyes laughed. A sound that could have been something like applause rippled down the bar and through the room of the tavern. The small man puffed out his thin chest.

"They told us," the woman said. "He was a good lawyer. He did very well in New York. We lived down near Grammercy Park. New York is a big city. The other men in his office were very nice to us, polite. But I never did see where any of them lived, their homes. After a while it got to him. They came to our place sometimes, most of them anyway, but they never invited us. I suppose they lived in the suburbs, that makes it hard. Today they'd invite us, once maybe or twice a year, things get better. It got to him, Tony. When you're young enough there's a lot to do in New York. We were fine until the drinking started. A lawyer has to be sober. I guess I hid it at first, I don't do that any more. He's a drunk, all right. Drunkie Tony, the lawyer who stokes boilers because it got to him and he drinks and his family paid him off. When he's sober, it's not bad."

They laughed, the people in the tavern, and stepped away from the bar so that they could see the small man better. At the tables they stood up to look. Those who seemed to know the small man pointed him out to those who had heard the shout but had not seen just who had shouted. Where he sat with the woman he could tell that most of the people in the bar knew the small man. They were not surprised, most of the people in the tavern, and the few strangers were having their questions answered by many people at the same time. The woman moved her slender hand on her beer glass and looked at no one in particular. The small man himself swayed where he leaned against the bar. He, the small man, brushed his hand against the air and grinned.

"I HATE NIGGERS!"

Preened like a peacock, the small man, his thin chest puffed out with the effort of his shout, his eyes blinking in the smoke, his slack lips loose in a grin as he turned his grey head right and left to accept whatever accolade would come. The people of the tavern only laughed, picked up their glasses, returned, already, to their drinks, their own affairs and conversation.

"Most of them don't know me," the woman said. "They'd be embarrassed. His father brought us back here. He said he needed a lawyer in the business. I suppose he wanted to try, the old man, but he died. Tony was a drunk, so they paid him off. It's his hometown, and a drunk's a drunk anywhere. I can work here, too. It's not really so bad when the woman is black. Marriage is going too far, but at least they don't feel cheated. When the woman is white then the men feel cheated, but when the man is white it's not so bad for them. They explain it. What white woman would marry a drunken bum? For drunks and cripples a nigger woman is okay, right boy?"

He would have answered, but the woman was not looking at him even now. She was looking toward the bar where the small man had closed his eyes, swayed, slipped against the bar, almost fallen on the floor. The woman stood up, took her purse, and walked toward the bar. He saw that she was taller than he had realized, taller than the small man, and her hips curved beneath the green dress that was wrinkled across her hips because it was a cheap dress and she had been sitting at the table for a long time. The small man opened his eyes and saw her. The small man tried to turn.

"Come on, honey," the woman said.

The small man reached out to the woman and took her by the arm. He swayed, held her arm. The brown skin of her arm turned white where his thin, hard fingers gripped her. Unsteady with his back away from the support of the bar, the small man pushed the woman before him toward the door out into the street. Stiff-legged, yet weak and loose, the small man stumbled toward the door, held to the woman, moved that way, half-supported and half-pushing, until they were slowly across the tavern, through the door someone held open, and out on the sidewalk that bordered the highway. On the sidewalk the small man stopped. The woman stopped. The small man pushed the woman. He pushed hard, sudden. She fell. She sprawled on the sidewalk in front of the open tavern door. The green dress bunched up around her waist. She lay with her thighs exposed to the blue and yellow neon of the tavern signs.

"God damn you!" the small man said.

The woman lay where she had fallen. The small man turned and walked back toward the tavern door. People stood in and around the open door. The bartender pushed his way through the people and stood in front of the small man. The small man swayed, blinked his thin eyes at the bartender who blocked his way. His neck bent, head forward, the small man peered into all the faces turned blue and yellow by the neon signs. The small man stepped toward the bartender. A short step, and another, trying not to sway, trying to stand straight as he smiled up at the bartender. The bartender reached out with one hand to touch the chest of the small man. The bartender pushed lightly against the small man's chest. The small man staggered backward, his foot striking the woman where she lay, almost tripping over the woman. The small man regained his balance and began to kick the woman.

"God damn you. Damn you. God damn you. Damn. Damn. Damn. . . ."

The woman made no move to escape the kicks, but raised one arm to break their force, to ward off those wild kicks that struck toward her face. The small man cried as he kicked at her. Two men walked from among the people at the tavern door and pulled the small man away from the woman. The small man stumbled away into the night, his thin figure a shadow passing beneath the dim street lights beyond the blue and yellow neon glare before the tavern. The two men helped the woman to her feet. She thanked the two men. She walked after the small man into the darkness. As she walked she held her side where some of the kicks had struck her. The two men rejoined the other people who all began to drift back into the tavern. The bartender closed the tavern door.

The night outside the tavern, where he stood on the sidewalk and watched the woman walk away, became quiet and still with few cars passing on the highway. His leg had begun to hurt from sitting so long with the leg bent beneath the chair at the woman's table. Inside the tavern the juke box began to play again. There was the sound of laughter and loud voices. On the highway two cars passed going in the wrong direction. In the beams of their headlights he saw the woman. She was still holding her side as she walked. He picked up his suitcase and followed her. When she turned from the highway, he followed down the dark side street past the isolated street lamps.

Away from the noise and neon of the tavern the night was quiet. Houses and many tall apartment buildings emerged from the night as he walked. In a few houses there were lights to show that some people were still awake at this early morning hour. He followed the woman across two more streets and into a wider street that was parallel to the highway. The few passing motors on the highway seemed far off. Ahead, the woman walked up some steps into the darkened entrance alcove of a tall apartment building that appeared to be part of a city project. There was no light in the entrance alcove. The woman disappeared as if into a tunnel.

He stopped across the street from the entrance to the building. He rested his suitcase on the sidewalk and waited for the light that would show that she had opened the door and gone into the building. No light came, and he picked up his suitcase and limped across the street. Only three windows in the tall building showed light at this hour. He looked up at the windows of the building to see if a light would go on to show where she lived. No light went on. He stood close to the dark entrance alcove and waited for her window to show light. After a time, when only the same three windows showed light in the building, he reached into his pocket for a match. He struck the match on its cover and held it out before him toward the dark alcove at the top of the short flight of steps.

He saw the face and green eyes of the woman. The small man was with her. They were sitting on the floor of the entrance alcove. They were far back near the unopened door into the building. The entrance was dingy, and there should have been a light, in the entrance and in the hallway inside the building through the half-glass door, but there was no light. The woman sat with her back against the entrance wall. The small man sat beside her and was held close against her by her arms around him. In the brief light of the match the woman's lips were moving as if she were singing. The match burned out. He reached into his pocket for another match, and took one step up the short flight of steps.

"Get away from here, boy."

In the darkness her low, hoarse, hard voice had no direction. It could have some as quick and sharp from anywhere in the night.

"I didn't come for that," he said.

"Go to New York, boy."

"I want to help," he said, and said again, "I didn't come for that."

"What else can you do for me, boy?"

He could not see her where she sat in the dark alcove holding the small man, but her voice was sharp and clear, and he waited for her to speak again. She said nothing more. Instead, she began to sing. Her song was low and almost toneless. He did not recognize the melody, and he could not hear the words, but the song had the soft, undulating rhythm of a lullaby. As he listened he became aware of a faint sound of movement inside the alcove. Movement that seemed to keep time to the rhythm of the song. After a minute or two he realized what it was. She was rocking the small man in her arms as she sang there on the floor of the dingy entrance alcove.

He picked up his suitcase and limped away. He walked back along the same side streets of trees and darkened houses until he reached the highway. He sat down on his suitcase at the side of the road. There were few cars passing now. He waited over an hour for a ride. The car that stopped to pick him up was an old Chrysler. This driver was a tall, lean man.

"Going far?" the driver said.

"New York."

"I'll take you through Albany," the driver said. "That's my home, Albany. Been away a week, and couldn't wait for tomorrow to get home. You live in New York?"

"No," he said, and said, "Just a visit. I've never been to New York. I thought I'd like to see it."

"Must be hard hitching with that leg," the driver said.

"It's not so bad," he said.

"I knew a guy who lost both legs under a train," the driver said. "Worked for the Central. Got a good settlement. After a while he learned to get around fine, too."

He leaned his head back against the car seat. The highway from Syracuse to Albany was long and dark. At this hour there were no distant lights in farmhouses. The towns were silent with dim street lamps. The porches were deserted. Only the all-night diners were open and lighted like isolated outposts in a dark jungle.

John W. McReynolds

who teaches at Dyke College in Cleveland, is the son of a regular Army officer and studied in Louisiana, and at Virginia Tech and the University of North Carolina. The author of *How To Plan For College and What to Do When You Get There*, Mr. McReynolds has contributed to *American Journal of Physics*, *Bulletin of the Atomic Scientists*, and has served on the staffs of the Baton-Rouge *State-Times* and *Morning Advocate*, and has reported extensively for midwest newspapers on the Congo, which he has visited several times.

A memo to the current madness

FOR SOME reason nobody, black or white, seems willing to talk out loud, to tell all the truth as it really is, and to say it so people can hear it; nobody, anyhow, who lays any claim to liberal respectability.

What is it all about? What did the white American do to the black American?

Well, for one thing, we bought you. Those God-fearing New England sailors, knew a good thing and they saw one, and you were it. Those Proper Bostonians who would later give us Harriet Beecher Stowe and *The Atlantic Monthly,* bought you and sold you, and they got the *money* and the South got *you.* The damnyankees had a racket better than wooden nutmegs and damn near as honest.

For another thing, we bred you like cattle.

If the South had only looked ahead, we could have raised up some of the best football talent in the country, which we did anyhow, and we could have kept it for our own use instead of shipping it off to the Big Ten and their having to send up into Clarion County, Pennsylvania to import a bunch of Catholics like we do now.

And for another, we burned you from time to time (or at any rate and what is worse, we allowed others to burn you) and whether this was for your edification or our amusement, I am not prepared to say. You were burned.

But these things, and the other things, were just minor manifestations of what we really did . . . the horror part. What we really did was this:

Everywhere we could, including in our Constitution which is now your Constitution too, we *thought* "nigger" even when we couldn't bring ourselves to say it or to write it. We kept it up until finally we got enough of you and enough of us to believe it.

Nigger? A nigger is somebody who thinks he's a nigger.

We kept it up, we called you nigger until you believed it and then we figured maybe we wouldn't have to bother with you anymore. We figured wrong.

Look back a minute—way back, and not in anger.

Real chains and leg irons and auction blocks weren't nearly so bad as what came after, and it is important that everybody see this. After all, if somebody owned you, you knew who he was. But who is The Man? Who is Mister Charlie? Slavery was just ordinary business, and not too much different from today's gray flannel slavery. The crime wasn't slavery. The crime was the thing that came afterwards, the thing that made niggers.

What we did was to kill your spirits and did it so neatly and softly and gently that we were able to keep those black bodies around to chop the cotton and eat the watermelon and generally see to it that the work got done. The bodies stayed alive, zombie-like. There was no *corpus delicti*. It was the perfect crime. Tell him he's a nigger until he believes it and maybe you do too, and then you got yourself a nigger. It's a lot more useful than a corpse.

The people who came late to this country are not the villains of the piece. They came over here, and steerage at that, which was not much better than the slave ships, and there wasn't anybody waiting to buy them except the politicians. They wanted to be rich, free Americans where the streets were paved with gold. They had a new language to learn and an old accent to forget. They wanted to join the club, to be All-American. So when they saw us calling black people "niggers" they picked up the habit. The crime wasn't theirs. All they did was go along with a bad joke.

But it's us, the ones who have been here as long as you and longer, the ones who did the destroying—we're the ones who know what it's about because we're the ones who did it. And *that*, my brother, is something it's getting harder to live with every day. It's a hopeless kind of knowledge, because we know what the problem is and we know what the answer is, but we can't do anything about it. We made the niggers, and now we're stuck with them.

Tell me—Do you think you can forgive us? And do you think you can make us clean just by forgiving us?

You are an albatross around my neck. You are a monkey on my back. I am the slayer and you are the slain, and that makes us real close down deep inside. We have got ourselves a relationship.

And whether we ask for forgiveness or not, you are going to have to forgive us anyhow, and I would hate to be in your shoes and facing something like that in the morning because it is going to take one hell of a lot of doing. But you're going to have to do it, because we are an albatross around your neck, too. You're going to have to live with yourself just like I'm going to have to live with myself.

And before either one of us can think about living, there's an awfully big pile of feces that's going to have to be shoveled out of the way before it smothers all of us.

We've all got to quit pussy-footing around and telling lies, and we've got to quit making up useful ways to pretend things didn't happen. There is no sense in trying to pretend the Constitution has really been strong for the black man all along and was just misunderstood by the learned judges until *Brown vs. Topeka Board.* We have to start from the truth, which is what I've been talking about.

And the rest of the truth? You've got to get rid of the niggers.

And how do you do that? Just the way you're doing it—some of you, little by little and slowly but surely. The day that lady on the bus in Montgomery just by God had enough . . . that's a day that has to come for everybody. Nobody gives it to anybody. Those that want it take it. Like Medgar Evers, who took his life in his hands every time he walked a step or spoke a word and died like Colin Kelly.

That poor black scratching red dirt for The Man, can't hardly read or write or figure or do a damn thing except follow his mule. You can go down there and stand by him and show him what's possible. I can go down there and tell him no one will burn him for voting or going to Church. But that's *all* we can do. The big thing, the big step, that's for him, and nobody can take it for him. That's where living is like dying for him, because he's all by himself. I guess maybe everybody's living is like dying, that way . . . the loneliness. From where that share-cropper stands—and he's a nigger and he stinks and don't forget it—from where he stands that's a long and lonesome road he's looking down, and he's got to walk it the whole way.

That day when he realizes or discovers or just plain flat out *decides* he's had a belly full of being a nigger and is going to be a Negro—that's the day when there will be something happening inside his own belly, starting with his own heart and tearing his own soul every which way but loose.

It's tough and it's hard and it's bitter, and it doesn't make me feel good about any of it. I told you, this is my problem, too. I've got a stake in it, just like you do and just like he does . . . if not for me, then for my kids and your kids and his kids.

As long as there's just one nigger left in this country it means that every time I look down into my own heart I see that rotten slimy mess there like screw-worns in my stomach and I can't stand it any more and I can't do anything about it.

It's your move.

You think you've had it tough? What do you think it has been for *us*? And when I say "us" I don't mean the whole country . . . you know who I mean. Not the liberals . . . not the do-gooders who are too nicey-nice to say *nigger* . . . not those big-hearted New Englanders who imported you. I'm talking about *us*. The ones who did it to you and then tried to turn our backs. We didn't kill your bodies . . . we killed your souls. And you know what the price you have to pay for that is? You remember about *An eye for an eye and a tooth for a tooth?*

That's the truth.

You want your so-called civil rights? You want your manhood? All right, then, damn it, come and get 'em.

But hurry. Please hurry.

All you want is your manhood. *Me, I'm waiting to get my soul back.*

And it's all up to you.

G. C. Oden

has had poetry appear in *Saturday Review* and other literary publications for a number of years. She has held Yaddo and Whitney Fellowships and a Breadloaf Scholarship. In addition to her poetry, she is a syndicated columnist.

Man white, brown girl etc.

Upon the Occasion of his Marriage

It is essential I remember
ours was a fair exchange.
We were a happy consequence
to paths of darkness
in a world
no less terrible or strange
for all our years of toiling
through it.

I valued you for what I took.
That burning in you bright
illumined our collision;
your phosphoresence still
must be reckoned with
when night
heretic with your memory
trespasses my lair.

God knows we were; and though such love
did not a kingdom come to us,
each the other's
wood of destiny
has lit.
You found your clearing:
I fathom mine.
We have had the best of it.

Poetry Northwest
Autumn, 1963

Paul Olsen

a Breadloaf Scholar in 1960, has appeared in the *Virginia Quarterly Review*, the *Texas Quarterly*, the *Southern Review* and *Cosmopolitan*. He is the author of the *Virgin of San Gil* and of the forthcoming *A Country of Old Men*, both novels.

Line of duty

THE JEEP slushed to a stop, its right side tilted slightly in a water-filled ditch along the road. The driver switched off the lights and pushed the barrel of his carbine at the hunched Negro sitting next to him. Feeling the sharp prod in his ribs, the Negro sprawled one leg over the side and dropped to the ground. The corporal scrambled out from the narrow back seat, stretched, and pushed the Negro over the ditch into the flat, cropped field; there was a scurry of cricket chirps and the corporal jumped on one foot.

"Damn."

The driver walked around the side of the jeep, vaulted the ditch, and came alongside the others.

"Go ahead," he told the Negro.

They walked across the field, soft and furrowed by the Korean rains, stumbling every few paces. The driver cursed softly and lurched against the corporal.

The Negro breathed deeply; the acrid odor of the human fertilizer plucked at his nose until he carefully sorted the smells like someone choosing perfumes. He finally caught the scent of the green-growing plants somewhere off to the left and twitched his nostrils, savoring the familiarity of fields and trees and good dirt. He felt a hand tighten on his arm and he dreamed of the smell of wet leaves and swimming naked in a river.

"All right," the driver said. "This'll do."

The Negro opened his eyes, blinked, and saw a thousand small shadows of shoots spring up all over the field in jagged irregular rows, probably sown by hand, scattered from a shoulder bag. Somehow the moonlight was painful. He looked up and saw the sparse foliage of a crooked tree that looked like a thick spider web against the grey clouds hanging low in the sky. He strained his neck toward the fields, listening attentively to the atonal crickets and the fantastic black bugs with the red collars that made parrot noises. He slumped against the tree trunk and looked back to the jeep; the faroff silhouette posed tilted drunkenly on the brink of the ditch.

"What are you going to do, B.L.?" the corporal asked, and bent, drawing his hand across the ground. He plucked the small stalk of a weed, made a sucking sound, and put it in his mouth, wedging it in the tiny space between his front teeth.

"I guess kill 'im," B.L. drawled, and flipped the carbine about a foot in the air, catching it by the stock. He jammed it under his armpit, took out a cigarette and struck a match against a stone. He held the match under the Negro's nose, looked straight into his face, then shook his head. "Christ alljesus," he said, "he's black as a coal mine."

He lighted the cigarette and threw the match away, puffing quickly until the end of the cigarette was long and glowing. He handed it to the corporal.

"You steamed it," the corporal said peevishly. "Like always."

The Negro, still leaning against the tree, closed his eyes again and dreamed of plunging his hands into the soft dirt, fondling it, watching it burrow into the soft flesh under his fingernails, bringing it up to his face to smell. Good ground if you could stand the smell of the manure. There's something to say for it, though, he considered analytically. It grows big; bigger than anything back home.

The corporal began to throw small rocks into the field; the bugs cricked defensively as each stone thumped into the brush. B.L. said:

"My old man told me when I was little—he told me they used to cart off big bunches of coons down to a place they called the hollow. They used to take 'em down there and cut 'em up real fancy so they couldn't even rape mules. Daddy said it was the best thing for 'em 'cause that way they couldn't even think of white women, you know." He paused and scratched his head, then looked pensive and snickered. "They yelped somethin' fierce," he said nostalgically. "Damn near drove 'em nuts." He looked toward the Negro. Then:

"That's a prize idea. I'd sure as hell like to take a whack at it if I wasn't scared of gettin' the clap. They born with it, you know. You can't go messin' around with niggers 'less you know how 'cause you'll get somethin' for sure. That's why white folk so scared of 'em. When they hop white women it's all over—it's like a sickness."

The corporal giggled softly and turned his back. He took out a handkerchief and blew his nose, the sound cutting through the field like a small muffled explosion.

"Cut them off," he said, and giggled again.

B.L. faced the Negro.

"How'd you like that, you friggin' cornhead? That's one more way you can go so close your eyes a bit and give it a real think."

The Negro nodded slowly and thought about castration: he almost laughed but kept his face taut, a mask without expression, and rested his head against the tree. He smelled the earth again and stretched his fingertips to feel a strong steel plow that could slice whole chunks from the fields. There was a long flat patch of plain green grass: it wasn't used for anything, not even pasture land, and when you were tired you stopped for a moment, wiped your forehead on your sleeve, and just looked. Suddenly you'd feel cool when you watched the bluish tint of the grass gleaming wet in the morning sun. It went off like the symmetry in a picture, way off until all you could see was a tiny rusty-red barn sitting alone on the horizon. You'd have killed the first cow that wanted to spoil it; because you built dreams on it, impossible dreams. You owned it.

"You know what I think I'll do? Think I'll rub the butt of this here rifle over his face so's he can't shave a month."

B.L. walked to the tree and placed his hands flat on the trunk, trapping the Negro's head in the basket of his arms. He stared intently, trying to make his eyes fierce, and screwed up his face into a snarl. The Negro snapped his head away, thumping it lightly against the trunk.

"You been doin' me wrong ever since you come to the company. Seems to me I told you before, but it looks like you need another lesson. You friggin' people been comin' in the army like you was part owner. You been livin' like a white man since you been in and nobody's said nothin' much about it. But you got to do things even a white man wouldn't do. You big wheel, ain't you?"

Suddenly he seized the Negro's shirt and twisted the collar into a ball. He pulled forward until their faces almost touched.

"I laid claim to that woman, you hear? She been mine since I been here and I don't want no man to touch her, 'less alone a nigger. You people get one look at white meat and you got to have it. You hungry, ain't you? You think 'cause she's a gook it don't matter. Well it does, cornhead. She ain't black and she mine, you hear?"

He released the collar and squatted, fondling the barrel of the carbine, whispering inaudibly. He removed a small bottle from the pocket of his shirt, drank, then corked it and passed it to the corporal, saying:

"Man, war is hell and you ain't just kiddin'."

The Negro turned his head slowly against the tree and bit his lip, then his tongue, fighting his smile. His woman. Just like my woman. He shook his head sadly. First woman you ever had and she's yours. You make real love, don't you? And she's hot, right? She doesn't give a flying damn whether you live or die, but she's yours. He wants her and she wants his Sears and Roebuck catalogue with all the pretty pictures of summer dresses and lace-edged underwear.

They heard the clanking drone of a truck winding around a bend toward the jeep. As the headlights struck the jeep it stood out darker, then disappeared when the truck rumbled past. B.L. slumped lower and winced as the truck seemed to stop, changed gears, then rolled further down the road.

"MP's."

"They don't use trucks."

They watched the tail light vanish in the darkness. B.L. sighed, rose, and brushed the dirt from his trousers. He took a clip of ammunition from his pocket and rammed it into the carbine. He clicked off the safety and lurched forward, his legs wide apart.

"I'm goin' to blow his head off right now."

"You talk like a fool, B.L. You could hear a shot a hundred miles away. It's too goddamn quiet to shoot. You got a knife?"

"No I ain't."

They began to whisper together, lighting cigarettes and blowing the smoke in the air. The Negro's stomach panged at the smell of the smoke and he licked his lips. He almost smiled again: castration without a knife. B.L.: a man without a name, only initials.

The corporal emptied the bottle and threw it into the field; it smashed on a rock, scattering the bugs, causing them to shriek unhappily.

"Well Christ," he said, "I'm not going to sit out here all damn night and catch pneumonia. You better think of something."

"What's the matter—ain't you got no brains? What am I, the friggin' ringleader?"

"It was your idea, hotshot. You got the gun, the bottle, and the smokes. You might as well have the brains too."

"Shut your mouth," B.L. said, waving the carbine over his head.

"Here, you'd better unload that thing before it goes off."

The Negro heard the click of the ammunition clip. The corporal examined the carbine carefully and took a step back.

"You sure there's nothing in it?"

"Goddamn, I took it out, didn't I?"

"Look in the chamber."

"What you think I am, an owl?"

"Give it here."

The corporal took the carbine, turned it over in his hands, and strained his neck forward to peer into the chamber. He squinted, twisting the stock in his hands again, holding it perpendicular, then horizontal to the ground.

"Can't see a thing," he said, and cursed. He locked the safety and handed the carbine to B.L. "Don't fool with it any more."

The Negro thought of the bottle and swallowed, feeling the dry sharpness stab at the back of his mouth. He wanted a beer: ice cold with no foam that you could pour into your stomach without tasting the bitterness. There was an old store, sagging under rotting clapboards and cracked shingles, that sold beer stored away in an ice house. Bottles you never saw in any state of the union: tall with scrawny necks, short-fat with stubby necks. No labels. Terrible stuff except when your thirst burned like a blue fire and the water was tepid like a sunny lake. Making hollow whooping noises by blowing sideways into the necks, all the old black men laughing and trying their damndest to play tunes. You bought a bottle for a dime, spending fifteen minutes searching through the maze of shapes, nursing your thirst until it almost seared a hole through your tongue. Then you grabbed one, bit the cap off, shook it so the foam belched out, and gushed it down, almost strangling, feeling as if little chinks of ice were coating your insides; and watching you, one of the old men groaning, *Boy, now you know what livin' is.* You struggled out the dime and laid the bottle carefully in a cardboard box like a dead friend. One was enough because it tasted like turpentine, but you weren't thirsty any more and you wouldn't be for hours until the sun fell and the water was cold. That is, if you survived the beer.

The Negro squinted his eyes in the darkness; he felt a drop of rain on his face and turned, watching the two men—only shapes now that the moon had gone—looking up toward the black sky. The corporal held his hand out and waited until he felt the rain.

"Oh Christ," he groaned.

The Negro squatted on his heels and smiled, sure that they had forgotten him. He laughed softly as they stared into the sky as if they had never been caught in the rain before. B.L. shifted his gaze to the top of the tree and mumbled something, then belched. He made a muffled sound through his nose and turned his head back to the carbine.

"So what?" he said. "What's a little rain? Got to figure out what to do with the coon."

He caressed the rifle, switched it from hand to hand, felt the screws and bulges with his fingertips; he smoothed one hand across the stock in an even, slow motion. The corporal said:

"You going to sleep with it or take it apart?"

"Mind yourself. I'm givin' this a good think."

The corporal lighted a cirgarette and looked at the Negro. He spat, picked up a pebble, and threw it at the tree.

"Who said you could sit? Get up off your ass so we can watch you. Like as not you'll run off somewhere with the gooks."

The Negro rose slowly, hearing the crack of his knees, and leaned back against the tree. The raindrops, falling on his face and neck, were needle-cool. He breathed deeply again until he felt the pressure in his lungs, closed his eyes, and put out his tongue to catch the rain. The fields began to give off a sweeter smell as if the rain were a disinfectant, washing away the latrine stink of the fertilizer.

"You better figure fast," the corporal said. "I'm not going to sit out here in the goddamn rain forever."

B.L. grunted, got up, and walked toward the tree. He took the Negro's ears in his hands and rocked his head lightly back and forth against the trunk. Then he let go and shook his head.

"You a friggin' problem, sambo. I can't figure out how you goin' to go. You black—maybe you gone already."

The Negro stared ahead. *They never touch you: they never come near you unless they're mad or forgetful.*

B.L. poked the carbine barrel under the Negro's adam's apple and played his finger across the trigger housing. He pumped his finger back and forth on the trigger, then gave the rifle a slight push. He turned and half flopped on the ground. The corporal watched him closely, quizzically, then hunched his shoulders and sighed, stuffing his hands into his pockets.

"Well?"

"Don't bitch no more. Rain's stopped."

"You want to beat him up a little?" the corporal said. "At least let's do something. We're out here to rough him up and we're getting the worst deal."

"You like my mother," B.L. grunted. He turned to the Negro,

letting the carbine fall across his thighs. "Why in hell you join the army? We used to have it knocked, you know? A good deal until they let you people in. Now we got it lousy and you never had it so good." He paused and looked reflectively at the rifle. "Man, you think I like to go in the same shower room with you? Bad enough I got to sleep in the same tent." He slapped his leg and expelled air from his mouth. "I don't know," he groaned. "That's the thing of it."

"He joined the army to see the world," the corporal said.

"He didn't join no army. Niggers are dumb but they ain't that dumb. Besides, if he joined they'd of stuck him in a coon brigade."

"There aren't any coon brigades. This is the modern army."

"The hell you say. Whole stockade's a coon brigade. They lock 'em up soon's they join just to get 'em used to it."

A dull lightning glow powdered the sky, playing over the plump clouds, igniting their tips. The small hulk of the jeep flashed a moment, then melted back into the darkness.

"Throw that gun down," the corporal said, "or you'll get struck."

"You always cryin'. You scared, go home."

"Look, you dragged me out to beat up some nigger I never even saw before, and you just sit here talking yourself out. If you're going to kill him, why go right ahead. If you're not, please go back to the jeep and we'll cut out. The next time you want to kill somebody, you better lay a plan when you're sober."

"Hold your water. When I'm ready to kill 'im I'll let you know. If you ain't satisfied why don't you start walking?"

The corporal grumbled and slouched down with the small of his back propped against the tree. The Negro watched the whiteness of his neck and flexed his fingers, feeling the strength of their tendons. He folded his hands behind his back and began to whistle a tuneless air.

"Maybe we should sing *Bringing In The Sheaves*," the corporal muttered.

"You mad?"

"Me? Hell no. Why should I be mad. Picknicking's fun this time of night." He paused a moment. "Say, why don't you string him up? I'll go get the jeep, see? He can stand up on the hood and maybe he can say a last word and a prayer. Then I'll count to three, you can shove it into first and take off like a big-ass bird." He lighted a cigarette and played with the burning match until it flickered out. "But you probably haven't got a rope," he added.

"You funny. Awful funny."

The corporal rose and kicked viciously at the tree, barely missing the Negro.

"Jesus Christ, do something, will you? You're acting like you love the nigger. Crap or get off the pot."

"Wait. Just wait. Let me think."

The Negro licked his lips, feeling the thickness roll up like a ball under his tongue. He felt the tongue with his fingers: fat, dry. He moved the tip slowly around his mouth trying to start a flow of saliva. He bobbed his adam's apple up and down, then gave up. He thought about the beer again, but suddenly it disgusted him and he wrinkled his nose. He wanted water from a well. Silvery clean, smelling like cut grass: sweet.

He wished that a family of Koreans would walk by, nonchalantly, dragging fifteen or twenty children along. Both of them would sprawl on the ground, shaking, cursing, and the corporal would moan. He bent, picked up a rock, and threw it with a quick jerky movement into the field. Some twigs snapped; the crickets howled and the two men fell to the ground breathing hard.

"You made me empty the friggin' gun," B.L. whispered.

The corporal sniffed and surveyed the field from eye level. He moved his head slowly from side to side, straining his ears to hear the snapping of the twigs that would not come again. Then he rose and paced furiously around the tree; he stopped and jerked B.L. to his feet.

"I'm not going to walk back so you're coming with me. I'll be goddamned if I'm going to stay here in the dark any more." He stopped talking and waited. "You coming or not?"

"I guess."

"Well go do something to the nigger and let's go."

B.L. walked to the Negro, swaggering, brandishing the carbine in the air like a saber. He clutched the Negro's collar again.

"I was goin' to kill you, cornhead, but I changed my mind. I kind to dumb animals and I goin' to let you off. But 'fore I go, just listen to what I got to say."

"Oh, Lord," the corporal groaned.

"You got to follow a few rules of the game, man. One, you ain't goin' to the barroom no more. Two, you ain't goin' near my woman no more. Now if you wise up you'll pay me some mind. If you don't I ain't just goin' to scare you no more, you hear?"

The lightning flashed again, this time sharp and clear directly overhead. Thunder sounded and the rain began to pour down in spurts. At first the stark branches of the tree held off the water, but the leaves overturned and it streamed down.

"Let's go, you dopey rebel," the corporal shrieked. He began to slam his hand against the tree trunk. "Jesus Godalmighty, please let's go."

"Okay, cornhead," B.L. shouted through the rain, "you walk from here." He prodded the Negro's groin with the rifle stock. "If you late for bedcheck, you ain't sayin' nothing', right? You ain't sayin' a friggin word."

Together, B.L. and the corporal ran back across the field toward the jeep. The corporal stumbled and screamed.

"Jesus H. Christ."

B.L. jerked him up and they scrambled into the jeep, almost chased by the hammering flashes of lightning. They gunned the motor and pulled off down the road. The Negro watched the tail light fade through the driving rain. Then he threw his head back until it hit the tree and laughed, the tears mingling with the rain on his cheeks. Suddenly he stopped laughing, shook his head mournfully, and pressed against the tree. He looked into the sky at the lighter shadows of the clouds, blinked, then started off across the field toward the road. He pulled the collar of his shirt up and smelled the air again. It was pure and odorless; even the smell of the plants had gone. He walked carefully, his eyes on the ground until he got to the ditch. He hopped it and stood in the road a moment looking back, trying to see the tree. The branches were dimly outlined against the sky: they swayed under the blanket of rain, making a vague swithing sound he hadn't heard before.

He thrust his hands into his pockets and waited, bowed in the rain, soaking up the water until he was wet through to his underwear. Then he began to walk slowly along the muddy road as if he had nowhere to go, shaking his head every so often to scatter the water that clung in drops to his hair.

A truck ambled in agony along the road in back of him. He stopped and stuck out his thumb. The truck passed, then slowed down and finally stopped, its front wheel close to the overflowing ditch.

Smiling, he ran toward the door that began to swing open.

Margaret Walker

a member of the English Department of West Virginia State College has been a social worker, newspaper reporter and magazine editor. She began writing poetry at the age of 13. She has been a lecturer at many universities including Iowa, Northwestern and Chicago. Her book, *For My People* was selected for the library of the Yale Series of Younger Poets.

Now

Time to wipe away the slime
from inner rooms of thinking,
and covert skin of suffering;
indignities and dirt
and helpless degradation;
from furtive relegation
to the back doors and dark alleys
and the balconies of waiting
in the cleaning rooms and closets
with the washrooms and the filthy
privies marked "For Colored Only"
and the drinking-soda-fountains
tasting dismal and disgusting
with a dry and dusty flavor
of the deep humiliation;
hearing vulgars shout to mothers
"Hey you, nigger, girl, and girlie!
Auntie, Ant, and Granny;
My old mammy was a wonder
and I love those dear old darkies
who were good and servile nigras
with their kerchiefed heads and faces
in their sweet and menial places."
Feeling hate and blood comingled
in a savage supplication
full of rites and ceremonies
for the separate unequal—
re-enforced by mobs who mass
with a priest of cult and klan
robed and masked in purest White
marking Kleagle with a Klux
and a fiery burning cross.
Time to wipe away the slime.
Time to end this bloody crime.

John A. Williams

is the author of *Night Song* and *Sissie*.
A fourth novel, *The Man Who Cried
I Am,* is to be published next year.
He is also the author of four non-fic-
tion works and many magazine arti-
cles, as well as television scripts. He
was for two years a contributor to
Book Week.

Navy black

(A Novel in progress)

DUST PUFFED in sudden transparent brown billows from beneath the wheels of the hurtling Jeep, sped upwards and slowed abruptly, then settled upon the broad leaves of the palm trees along the narrow coral road.

The two heavily tanned officers in the Jeep pressed their overseas caps down tightly upon their heads. They approached the hairpin curve and had to slow. Their diminished speed allowed them to see, fleetingly, a basketball game in progress upon a cleared, dusty coral court. The driver who had broken down into second as they rushed into the curve, gave the Jeep gas then shifted back into third. Bouncing fiercely now, they burst out of the curve and onto the calm green expanse of the compound of the 27th Special Naval Construction Battalion. The driver shifted back into second and picked his way down the neat roadway marked off by lumps of whitewashed coral, heading toward the CO's tent where the flag snapped back and forth in a hot wind. The area was quiet. Only the *clat, clattat, clit, clatclit, bling!* of a typewriter sounded above a few muffled voices. The officers climbed out and rubbed their perspiration-stained bottoms with their hands. They paused and looked up and down, then started up the steps to the CO's office.

Bright had been lying down when he heard the Jeep. It had come with such a rattling rush through that hot midday that he'd raised himself automatically to see. He propped himself up with an elbow. Who after all would be running like hell through a torrid Guamanian afternoon but officers or basketball players reliving their moments of high school glory? Bright stared at the neat, tight look of the two men. Unmistakably marines. Marines, Bright thought. They vanished through the CO's door. There were momentary hearty greetings. Bright lay back down, thinking, God, it's hot. It's too damned hot. He closed his eyes and sighed. Marines.

Something was crawling on his leg. With his eyes still he closed he wondered lazily what it was, if it were poisonous. He jerked his leg and the crawling stopped. Bright wondered if any other sackrats had seen the marines. He jerked his leg again, this time viciously; the crawling had begun again.

Young laughter. Bright opened his eyes. "Cut the crap, Frankie." The swaggering Chamorro boy laughed again and tossed his thick black hair out of his thin, ebony eyes. Bright stared at the boy's slight, exquisitely tanned Micronesian frame, so much more attractive than the hard black of the Melanesians in the Solomons or the weak paleness of the Polynesians in the Samoas. Bright sprang to his feet. "You come here and I'll kick your butt good, you little punk," he said. He threw the twig out upon the ground then flung himself back on his cot. Frankie walked around picking up pebbles, smiling close-eyed taunts at Bright. "I wish you would!" Bright said. "I wish you would throw those at me!"

"Aw," Frankie said tentatively, "shut up." He curled his full pinkish lips.

"Little bastard," Bright muttered so Frankie would not hear him. Then loudly: "You get away with murder around here." He glared at the boy and said softly, "Damned little gook."

Serious now, the boy approached the steps cautiously. "Where's Lyons?"

"He's a cook, isn't he?"

"Yes. . . ."

"Then he'd be in the kitchen where he always is, wouldn't he?"

Frankie opened his mouth to speak then closed it.

"And don't go around calling your father by his last name."

Frankie entered the tent and sat on Lyons' cot across from Bright. "He's no my father yet. What I call him?"

"I don't give a damn what you call him. If I was him I wouldn't adopt you; I'd leave you on this rock to rot."

Frankie sprayed the pebbles outside. "Bright, you mad for yesterday?"

"You're damned right I'm mad."

"Why you fellas no like that name when white fellas call you?"

Bright refused to hear him for several seconds. He fixed his gaze on the CO's door.

"Bright?"

Bright ignored him.

Frankie looked restlessly around the tent.

"It's not a nice name," Bright and finally. "It makes you fight."

"You mad yesterday when I say it, Bright?"

"Yes."

And Lyons, him mad too?"

"He should've kicked your butt," Bright said. He turned back to the CO's tent. "You like the white fellas better than the black fellas, huh, Frank?"

A faint shout went up from the basketball court. Bright felt sweat trickle from his armpits onto the cot.

"In America you'd be just like *us*; you wouldn't be like them. You aren't white and they'd soon make you know it."

"I not say I white."

"You act like it."

"I not." Frankie watched Bright's still, dark back.

"You think you're better than us already. Some colored guys in our outfit are *lighter* than you. Where do you get off?" Bright turned to the boy again. "Any white fellas offer to adopt you Frankie, like Lyons, and take you back to America?"

Frankie rapped his bare toes against the wooden floor.

"Did they!" Bright shouted.

Frankie jumped and edged toward the steps. Bright whirled to a sitting position. "Little *rat!* Come in here and take everything from Lyons—his money, his time, his love and then laugh at him behind his back—I've *seen* you—and call him names to his face— *get out—*" Bright charged to his feet, grasped the still thin elbow and pushed. Frankie tried to find his footing on the steps, scrambled, missed and fell, scurrying out of range in a thin cloud of coral dust at the same time, frightened. "Gook bastard," Bright growled. As soon as he was again on his back, staring at the crease of the tent above his cot, he knew it was all wrong. A patter of feet told him Frankie was no longer standing twenty feet away, staring at him, but running away as fast as he could.

Bright stared at the crease a long time. He heard the CO's door slam; he heard the voices and then the Jeep grinding down the road.

Frankie had been a nice kid at first; nice and grateful, the way you expected liberated kids to be. He minded then and was pleased with everything they did for him, like the clothes someone sewed together for him, sending food to his uncle, giving him money, teaching him clean habits, proving by their actions that he didn't have to be suspicious of them. *Damn him!* And then Lyons, small, fat, sweating all the time, his pocked brown face with a smile always, took him over, spoke of adoption, wrote his wife, for they could have no children. Then followed all the afternoons in the offices of ComSoPac or the Provost Marshal seeing about the endless required papers and permissions and the difficult conversations with the withered old uncle, toothless, grinning all the time.

Lyons climbed heavily up the steps. Bright knew it was him by his tread; Bright looked at him. Lyons had a soiled dishcloth around his neck; his skivvy shirt was so soaked with sweat that it too looked dirty. His white pants, stained with grease and spilled foods and sweat, hung soggily over his shoetops. "Hey, ol' buddy, did I hear Frankie 'round here a while ago?"

"Man," Bright said, "I don't see how come you don't lose some weight in all this heat. It's got to be worse in that kitchen." Bright turned on his side. "Yeah, your boy was here."

Lyons sat on his cot. "Whewww!" he said. "Doc, you see them marines?"

"Yeah."

"Another push, you think?"

"I don't know."

"Maybe they're thinking about Japan. Lot of brass up around ComSoPac these days. Besides them beaches down along the highway're packed with equipment.

"Don't be so cheerful."

Lyons stretched out on his cot with a pleasurable sigh. "Where's that damned boy? Got a letter from my old lady today, Doc. She thinks Frank's a pretty good-looking cat. Like me."

"Sure."

Lyons laughed.

"Think he'll like it?"

Lyons said, "Sure, he'll like it. Best damned country in the world."

Bright peeked at Lyons and saw that he meant it. "Yeah," he said.

"Things're lookin' pretty good with the papers, Doc."

"Oh yeah?"

"Another two or three weeks."

"Great."

"Wife's started to buy things already," Lyons said with a chuckle. "They'll be too small or too big. Hell, we might not get off this rock for another five years."

"You can say that again."

"Be good gettin' him used to the States. Always wanted a boy."

"Uh-huh."

"Oh, I know he's a little wild sometimes, Doc," Lyons said apologetically. "But I don't want no sissie boy. Frank lost all his folks but his uncle while the Japs were here. I mean, it's been hard on him."

"Yeah, I know."

"But you don't like him."

"I like him fine, Lyons, no crap."

"Naw you don't. You try, but you can't."

"Frank's all right with me. Honest."

Lyons said, "I guess I can handle a kid all right."

Bright sat up. "Lyons—"

"Ummm?"

Bright hesitated then lay back down. "What's for chow?"

"Es and Es."

"Christ."

"Chicken Sunday."

"Cut the crap. We have chicken *every* Sunday, just like turkey and mince pie for Thanksgiving and Christmas. It's a wonder we don't have a portable ice cream parlor for the boys."

"This is one of your good days."

"It was until those damned gyrenes showed up."

Lyons rose and stretched. He tapped his fingers against his sodden belly. "Time to get back. Trucks should be on the way. See Frankie tell him to clean up for supper."

"Okay."

Bright watched Lyons waddle back to the chow hall. On the way he passed the basketball players on their way to the showers at the edge of the compound. "You guys take your salt pills?" Bright called out.

They grinned and nodded and Bright knew they were lying. He watched them move nude, towels clutched in their hands toward the stalls. Their brown bodies glistened with sweat. "See those marines?" one of them called back.

"Knew it was too quiet after that Iwo push," another said loudly.

Bright lit a cigarette and lay smoking until he heard the trucks coming in. From this moment until after the movie there would be noise in camp; noise and music; voices cajoling, singing; voices raised in genuine and mock anger; crap shooting. There would be footsteps on crumbling coral walks; the somehow envious taunts thrown at those who would go down to the army engineers' camp looking for "Miss" Camel and his friends; Perry Como's voice, a prelude to the movie issuing from the PA from Armed Forces Radio.

Bright heard Roy singing, and when the husky, wide-shouldered man entered the tent, his Seabee baseball-type cap pulled low over his eyes, smelling of sweat which had dried in white rings on his shirt, Bright said, "You happy bastard, the marines were here looking for you."

Roy stopped singing. "What?"

"The guys from the First were here."

Roy stripped quickly to get to the showers before they became too crowded. "Jesus, I humped enough ammunition for those guys down on Peleliu to last them for fifty wars. I'm tired of white folk's wars anyway. What's the poop?"

"Haven't heard anything for real."

"Damn," Roy said, taking down his khaki towel and slipping his feet into wooden clogs. He draped the towel over one shoulder and with his cap still on, walked nude to the showers, muttering, "Home alive in '45. Crap."

II

The August morning was like any other; hot and breaking with the sun screaming bright shimmering gold off the Pacific east; shouts in the compound; the clatter of trays and stainless steel in the chowhall; the heavy thud of reluctant feet bumping the rails of the trucks. The morning sick call went quickly, as always, for the doctor a sullen, sneering, suspicious man with a great brush mustache and a sloping, bald head, his face, like his naked torso, ugly with atabrine color, did not like mornings. He peddled up and down the line in wrinkled khaki shorts, eyes puffed from the nights of drinks and nurses and Red Cross girls, seeking the malingerers; and when they complained of backaches, he gave them ruthless prostate massages and sent them to the waiting trucks, and they, loaded with Negro Seabees, groaned off the base on the way to the docks, while the small group of white Seabees turned to their office tasks.

All this to the incessant drone of the 24's and 29's circling high above, their silver bodies reflecting the shary rays of sun. The island filled and reverberated with the sounds of their engines; the sky was violated with aircraft. They made a final sweep around and headed west, joining the groups up from Tinian and Saipan. For many moments after they had gone, the silence that seemed to creep back in, like a thief, was hard to accept.

Bright tossed out foot basins of potassium permanganate solutions which had been used for fungus rinses. He worked quickly, envying bitterly the white corpsmen who had already returned to their beds or had gone off by Jeep or ambulance to the beaches. When he finished, Bright took a handful of chlorine pills used for purifying water, but which also bleached clothes, and dropped them in a bucket of water and soap. He placed soiled underwear in next and jabbed the mass tentatively a few times, then slid it under his cot. The cleaning detail sauntered by as Bright loosened his shoes before getting into bed.

"Doc, you got it made," one named Dixon said. He was so black they sometimes called him blue.

"I earned it," Bright said, inviting the daily exchange of repartee, but the sound of trucks, great two-by-tens grumbling up the road broke it off.

Marine trucks. Marine drivers wearing low-slung fatigue caps, giving them that tough white-boy look. A clerk in the CO's waved the vehicles down the road to the peeling quonset hut that served for storage. Curious, Bright strolled through the rows of tents, past the area where the white personnel lived, to the warehouse. He watched the marines and the cleaning detail, which had been pressed into service, unload.

Helmets. Gas masks. New fatigues. New shoes. New packs. New *weapons*. New, everything new. Where were the crosses that were usually loaded in the bows of ships, all strapped together, a couple of hundred crosses and three or four Stars of David? *Cholera vaccine,* some cartons in the last truck were stencilled.

"Hey, hey, Doc," Dixon said. "Does this stuff mean what I think it means?"

"Man, I don't know."

Dixon took a handful of helmets into the hut. "Know what happened the last time we got stuff like this?"

"Yeah."

"My eighteen months were just about up," Dixon said, grabbing another handful of helmet straps, rattling the helmets like buckets.

"So're mine," Bright said. He left the trucks and plodded back to the tent. Lyons lay on his cot, his eyes closed, but he spoke when Bright entered. "Seen Frank?"

"No."

Lyons stroked his forehead. "Wonder where he is?"

"New equipment's in."

"Saw it."

"I thought the damned war was just about over."

Lyons said, "I guess I'll have to get on over to his uncle's." He waited for Bright's answer.

"Hell, the kid's all right."

"You don't want to go with me?"

"No."

"Jesus, it's hot!" Lyons said, squeegeeing the sweat off his brow. "You hear about the new gun, the secret weapon?"

"What, another one?"

Lyons rose on one elbow. "All the battleships are being fitted with 'em, and when one of those special shells land, nothing'll grow there for a thousand years."

"Crap! Where'd *that* scuttlebutt come from?"

"The guys down at the docks."

"Look, if they had something special they'd a used it already, and they haven't used it which means they haven't got it. I mean doesn't that make sense?"

Lyons lay back down. "I don't know."

They didn't speak for several minutes, then Bright said, "Just wait until the guys get in at noon and see that stuff."

The Seabees bounded off the trucks before they rattled to a halt alongside the screened chowhall, and the chowline formed quickly. Most of the men would wait until after the meal to wash, if they did at all; some would eat rapidly and run for their cots and try to sleep for the balance of the hour they had in camp.

Bright leaned near the entrance thrusting his container of salt pills at each man.

"Hey, Doc, we off again?"

"What's the poop, Bright, we gonna invade Mississippi?"

"Man, will you quit shovin'—"

When Bright entered the hall, moving slowly along the clattering line, he saw Lyons standing as usual, overseeing the servers, one fist thrust into the fat of a hip, sweat dripping and spurting along the furrows of his forehead, falling in murky silver drops to the dirt floor. "Seen him?" Lyons asked.

Bright shook his head. "I'll let you know if I do."

Lyons nodded.

The hall buzzed. A "push" however much feared, shattered the monotony of the daily routine at the docks; that deadly, civilian-like employment so foreign to men who reluctantly anticipate once again the glamor of war.

But for Bright there was only the weary and frightening probability of packing up, herding aboard an APA to the catacombs of the various holds to be engulfed in the stink of men placed but a foot apart, stacked from top to bottom, hanging like stalactites in the gloom. The heads would run over and smell; the men would stand for quick, half-cooked meals in the ship's chowhall. During the days on deck there would be that interminable search for shade. There would always be the search for privacy; a fruitless search aboard an attack transport. And how many times a day on this one would there come the blowing out of the mike on the PA system, followed by the metallic:

"Now hear this!"

Undoubtedly there would be red and green and yellow alerts; hours of standing in the holds girded by cumbersome, reeking life jackets waiting for the planes to finish their business above, tiny and unreal in the dome of sky. And there would be times when they'd pile topside, still with those soiled and gritty life belts, standing away from the hatches waiting for the explosion of the torpedo, listening to the sea sliding past the bow, hissing all the way back into silence at the stern.

Then one fine morning the ship would rock with the waves and the sound of the screws would be absent and while you were wondering what that meant, as if you didn't know, the guns opened up, shattering at first, and then somehow conveying the idea of power and protection. Then up on deck, life belts behind, packs and guns and kits now; helmets too so that you looked like the fighters in the magazines. All over the sea there'd be a thousand other ships, but you noticed the DEs and DDs first; they would be small and fast and the sea would boil away from their bows as they charged the beach. *"Coxswains, man your boats!"* There would be the scrambling down the nets, the cough of the motors of a hundred landing barges moving in a line toward that distant soft green mound rising foolishly up out of the middle of the sea, stubbornly claiming a marking on the maps, a place in history. You would tell yourself that no enemy could survive the barrage; it helped to think that, until you reached the beach, called red or orange or blue, or some sillier color when it was really black volcanic sand or brown or white coral, and the

Roy rolled over and snapped it on. "Why the hell don't you buy garees, and chambray shirt and the blue denim pants. His white still forms of Americans would be lying there. Then you'd begin to feel naked and sacrificed.

"Bright. Bright!" the chief said, bending over the table. "Check out kits this afternoon. I think we might need a new supply of syrettes." The chief looked nervous. He was a fat, pink man with blue eyes and curly brown hair. He wore his khakis sloppily and drank a lot of beer and played a lot of cards, but he didn't press his corpsmen and stood between them and the doctor.

"When do we innoculate?" Bright asked.

"I guess tomorrow or the next day."

"So soon?"

"Yeah. Look," the chief said, straightening, "take care of those kits as soon as you can, will you, Bright?"

"Okay, chief."

The camp lapsed into a torpid silence when the last truck moved out. A Piper cub buzzed overhead. Bright sat in the shade checking the kits. The musty smell of the heavy cloth made the holds of ships suddenly more real to him.

Morphine syrettes, plastic caps securely fastened; ABDs (those great absorbent pads with straps, good for nearly any sized wound which left you still alive) sterile; Sulfa powders, —nilamide, —thiazole, —diazine, —pyridine, okay; tape, okay. Two by two, four by four bandages, sterile, okay. Bright locked up the kits and walked to the chief's tent passing two sunbathing clerks from the CO's office. Off duty chiefs sat around drinking beer, their caps and overseas hats off, the stark white upper parts of their heads showing. "Chief," Bright said, "we can use some more syrettes. Everything else's okay."

"Thanks, Bright. Take a cold beer. Go ahead."

Bright reached into the bucket filled with chipped ice and cans of beer. "Thanks," he said. One of the chiefs handed him an opener which he applied to the can; he sipped it as he walked slowly to his tent to sleep away the balance of the afternoon. He slept soundly, missing the return of the trucks, the shouting in the shower, the tip-toeing Roy, who, when he first saw Bright curled in sleep, sweating, decided he would not awake him for chow. This was a delightfully malicious decision; Roy had worked extremely hard on the docks; Bright seemed to have worked even less than usual. But Bright woke up and managed to get into the chowhall before it closed. Once hunched in the nearly silent hall over his food, listening to the KPs rushing to get through, he wondered why he'd bothered.

Back in the tent he stuck a stick in his clothes in the bucket under the cot, lifted the underwear out, changed its position and pushed it back to soak some more. Bright and Roy didn't go to the movies. Lyons had borrowed a Jeep and was off to find Frankie. As the tentmates lay unspeaking, the sounds from the movie drifted over the compound; voices and music. Bright could tell from the way the music went when something exciting was going to happen. Now the planes began to return from their strike; they always came back during the movies, drowning out both voices and music. Stacked up, they circled, their lights blinking frightened red and green dots in the dark blue of the sky.

An explosion lashed out against the night; a tongue of light seared the dark palms stark white for an instant, then the each ricochetted back and forth across the island as an uneven billiard ball rolling from cushion to cushion. The undersized, almost ludicrous wail of a siren came faintly.

Roy said to Bright, "I wouldn't think there's anything left. You?"

"Can't tell." Bright stared up at a spider spinning a web in the crease of the tent above his cot. He planned to kill the spider before he turned in.

"Saw one of those babies come down three months ago," Roy said. "Saw the guys in the bubble waving, glad to be setting down, smiling and then—*Towie!*" Roy paused.

"How about the radio?" Bright asked.

Roy rolled over and snapped it on. "Why the hell don't you buy one?"

"Because you got one," Bright said, getting up to kill the spider.

III

The trucks did not go out the next morning. Shouts of glee went up from this row of tents and that; faces were happy in the chowhall for the first time in months. The corpsmen ate a hasty breakfast and retreated to the sickbay to set up for the cholera innoculations. While they were setting up, the morphine syrettes arrived from the Fleet Hospital. Bright went out to meet the truck. "You get this?" the driver asked.

"Yeah," Bright said, lifting the carton out.

"You have to sign," the driver said. His cap was snow white and crimped down. His dungarees had been bleached powder blue. He wore an earring in his left ear, a large gold one.

"Where?" Bright asked.

"Anywhere," the Fleet corpsman said, "and date it."

"What's the date?"

"August sixth."

Bright scribbled and handed the pad back and took the carton into the hut. "Chief, here's the morphine."

"Lock it up with the kits, Bright." The chief was setting out the syringes and needles. The other corpsmen broke open the serum and set the medications tables with cotton, alcohol and check-off lists.

Lyons came by and stood in a corner. He had put on his dungarees, the chambray shirt and the blue denim pants. His white cap, a little soiled, sat squarely upon his head. He was sweating profusely.

"Find him yesterday?"

"No. Got to go back out today. Nice and cool in here," he said.

"Until you get used to it."

"Uncle hasn't seen him either," Lyons said.

"He'll show."

"I'm mad with him now," Lyons said. "That's no way for a kid to behave when you're going to adopt him."

"Maybe he doesn't want to be adopted."

"Sure he does, Doc."

"Okay."

Lyons said, "What makes you so sure?"

Bright shrugged but he wanted to remind Lyons of the fight between the Negro sailors at the Naval Advanced Base and the marines over the Chamarro girls at a party. One marine killed, thirty-nine sailors court-martialed for repulsing the attack. And Bright wanted to tell Lyons of the Chamarro girls who told you shyly that the white service men made them stay away from the black ones; and to recall for his friend the stories of tails and bayings at the full moon, and ask had not Frankie heard and seen? "Just a feeling," Bright said.

"Well . . . ."

"What's for chow tonight?"

"Stew."

"Stew! Well, what the hell are we having for lunch?"

"Spam sandwiches. I got to go," Lyons said, not moving.

"If I see him around here . . . ." Bright's voice trailed away.

Lyons started out. Stopped, turned. "Give me my shot now."

Bright motioned toward the chief and Lyons walked toward him, rolling up his sleeve.

Now the line began to form. Bright stood in a small line of corpsmen facing a longer line of Seabees, their arms exposed. First Bright swabbed, dashing on a splash of denatured alcohol for the next corpsman to hit with the needle. Then Bright went on the needle, hitting the arm swiftly, jabbing the plunger, withdrawing the needle from under a cotton ball and replacing that needle with another, sterile one for the next in that endless line of arms, each of which took one half cc of serum. "Work your arm!" he said automatically, "Work your arm!"

From the sickbay the line stretched through sun and shade to the warehouse to receive the new equipment, and when that was deposited in the tents, the toughening up exercises began, the running, the push-ups, the jogging. Cadence calls rang out, and then faded as the men jogged off to a nearby range to practice with the carbines and the rifles.

The chowhall was relatively quiet during lunch; the shots, the equipment, the feel and sound of the guns going off, made the men sombre. Going on another push was no longer a possibility; it was fearful, unexciting fact.

The men returned to the range after lunch and fired until almost chowtime. Bright, standing at one of the intervals the corpsmen had been set at, crept into position and took a carbine and fired with the rest. At Peleliu and Kwajalein he'd managed to carry a carbine in with him; it made him feel better. No one went to see the Van Johnson movie. He played out his role to a movie area empty of people. The Seabees lay in their beds or talked in the company streets. The bombers droned back home, vibrating the night.

In their tent, Roy turned on his radio.

"Thanks," Bright said. "You want to leave that with me?"

"You're goin' too, Bright, what the hell're you talking about?"

"I mean, leave it *to* me?"

"Shut up!"

"Sorry, didn't mean to make you nervous—"

At the same moment Roy hushed Bright, noise tumbled away from the entire camp, except for the movie. Radios, all tuned to the same station, delivered the message. When it was finished a shout went up around the camp. Roy turned to Bright grinning. "Did you hear *that*, man?"

Bright grinned. "Damned right I heard it."

"An atom bomb," Roy said. "What kind of bomb is that? Powerful as the sun."

"Hiroshima," Bright said.

"Surrender, bastards," Roy said, gritting his teeth. "You think they'll surrender?"

"I don't know."

"Surrender!" Roy walked around the tent pounding a fist into an open hand. "Surrender! Surrender!"

Lyons came in and sat heavily on his cot. Outside the shouts grew in intensity. They could hear beer spewing from punctured cans. There was running, and soon, singing. Voices were eager with hope. "Whew," Lyons said. "It's hot."

"Hear the news?" Bright asked.

"Yep."

"Find him?"

Lyons kicked off his shoes. "I found him."

Roy stopped walking and sat down, staring at the floor and then at his new equipment.

Dixon burst in. "The CO's called off everything for tomorrow!"

Roy gave him a smile.

"Yahooooo!" Dixon screamed, turning and racing for the next tent.

Lyons sat up suddenly and slipped on his shoes. "Doc?"

"What, man?"

"Step outside."

Roy looked quickly from Lyons to Bright. "What's wrong Lyons?"

Lyons ignored him and tied his laces. "You gettin' ready, Doc?"

Bright raised himself. "You serious?" Stepping outside had but one meaning. He saw that Lyons was serious.

"C'mon," Lyons said.

"Hey," Roy said.

"Listen, Lyons—" Bright said.

"I've already thought about it," Lyons said.

"What's this all about?" Roy asked, his arms swinging free at his sides, his chest swelling slightly.

"Frankie, I guess," Bright said, climbing slowly out of bed. He slipped on his shoes, took them off and put his sneakers on. "Ready in a minute," he said, glancing up at Lyons.

Roy said, "What about Frankie?"

"Tell him, Lyons."

"He's not going home with me," Lyons said, not looking at either of them." He said he thought about it after—" he gestured toward Bright "—talked to him." He hesitated, his eyes still on the floor. "He said he didn't want to go back and be like *us*."

Roy laughed harshly. "Well, you're lucky."

Lyons said sadly, "Shut up, Roy."

Bright stepped past them. Roy grabbed Lyons arm. Bright said, "It was my fault. Let him go."

"What'd you say?"

"I told the kid a little of how it was; he was always smart; he got the point."

"Aw, Lyons," Roy said. "That kid was so rotten; he was making a fool of you, man—"

Lyons shook loose and followed Bright down the steps.

"Oh, no!" Roy said, thrusting his powerful body between them. "Not over that kid. Lyons, what the hell did you think you were gonna do with him anyway? Boy, he'd run you and your wife outa house and home inside a week. I thought you'd wake up after a while." Roy had Lyons' arm again, holding tight and talking fast. The three stood alone. The night was filled with joyful running and shouting men.

Lyons started to cry. He turned away from them, and taking a soiled handkerchief from his pocket, wiped his eyes. He climbed back inside the tent, slipped off his shoes and lay down. Outside, Roy said to Bright, "Let's walk around and leave him alone for a while. He'll be all right."

"Sure," Bright said slowly, looking behind at Lyons as they moved down the company walk to where warm beer was being disbursed in celebration of what looked like the end of it.

Richard Wright

is the author of over a dozen books of which the most famous is *Native Son*. He was born in Mississippi in 1908 and died in Paris in 1960. Wright wrote of Africa, America and Spain (*Pagan Spain*) and after his death one of his early unpublished novels, *Lawd Today*, was published in New York, soon followed by *Savage Holiday*, originally published in 1954, and a new edition of *White Man, Listen!*

The plea

COURT OPENED and the judge said, "Are you ready to proceed, Mr. Max?"

"Yes, Your Honor."

Max rose, ran his hand through his white hair and went to the front of the room. He turned and half-faced the judge and Buckley, looking out over Bigger's head to the crowd. He cleared his throat.

"Your Honor, never in my life have I risen in court to make a plea with a firmer conviction in my heart. I know that what I have to say here today touches the destiny of an entire nation. My plea is for more than one man and one people. Perhaps it is in a manner fortunate that the defendant has committed one of the darkest crimes in our memory; for if we can encompass the life of this man and find out what has happened to him, if we can understand how subtly and yet strongly his life and fate are linked to ours—if we can do this, perhaps we shall find the key to our future, that rare vantage point upon which every man and woman in this nation can stand and view how inextricably our hopes and fears of today create the exultation and doom of tomorrow.

"Your Honor, I have no desire to be disrespectful to this Court, but I must be honest. A man's life is at stake. And not only is this man a criminal, but he is a black criminal. And as such, he comes into this court under a handicap, notwithstanding our pretensions that all are equal before the law.

"This man is *different,* even though his crime differs from similar crimes only in degree. The complex forces of society have isolated here for us a symbol, a test symbol. The prejudices of men have stained this symbol, like a germ stained for examination under the microscope. The unremitting hate of men has given us a psychological distance that will enable us to see this tiny social symbol in relation to our whole sick social organism.

"I say, Your Honor, that the mere act of understanding Bigger Thomas will be a thawing out of icebound impulses, a dragging of the sprawling forms of dread out of the night of fear into the light of reason, an unveiling of the unconscious ritual of death in which we, like sleep-walkers, have participated so dreamlike and thought-lessly.

"But I make no excessive claims, Your Honor. I do not deal in magic. I do not say that if we understand this man's life we shall solve all our problems, or that when we have all the facts at our disposal we shall automatically know how to act. Life is not that simple. But I do say that, if after I have finished, you feel that death is necessary, then you are making an open choice. What I want to do is inject into the consciousness of this Court, through the discussion of evidence, the two possible courses of action open to us and the inevitable consequences flowing from each. And then, if we say death, let us mean it; and if we say life, let us mean that too; but whatever we say, let us know upon what ground we are putting our feet, what the consequences are for us and those whom we judge.

"Your Honor, I would have you believe that I am not insensible to the deep burden of responsibility I am throwing upon your shoulders by the manner in which I have insisted upon conducting the defense of this boy's life, and in my resolve to place before you the entire degree of his guilt for judgment. But, under the circum-stances, what else could I have done? Night after night, I have lain without sleep, trying to think of a way to picture to you and to the world the causes and reasons why this Negro boy sits here a self-confessed murderer. How can I, I asked myself, make the picture of what has happened to this boy show plain and powerful upon a screen of sober reason, when a thousand newspaper and magazine artists have already drawn it in lurid ink upon a million sheets of public print? Dare I, deeply mindful of this boy's background and race, put his fate in the hands of a jury (not of his peers, but of an alien and hostile race!) whose minds are already conditioned by the press of the nation; a press which has already reached a decision as to his guilt, and in countless editorials suggested the measure of his punishment?

"No! I could not! So today I come to face this Court, rejecting a trial by jury, willingly entering a plea of guilty, asking in the light of the laws of this state that this boy's life be spared for reasons which I believe affect the foundations of our civilization.

"The most habitual thing for this Court to do is to take the line of least resistance and follow the suggestion of the State's Attorney and say, 'Death!' And that would be the end of this case. But that would not be the end of this crime! That is why this Court must do otherwise.

"There are times, Your Honor, when reality bears features of such an impellingly moral complexion that it is impossible to follow the hewn path of expediency. There are times when life's ends are so raveled that reason and sense cry out that we stop and gather them together again before we can proceed.

"What atmosphere surrounds this trial? Are the citizens soberly intent upon seeing that the law is executed? That retribution is dealt out in measure with the offense? That the guilty and only the guilty is caught and punished?

"No! Every conceivable prejudice has been dragged into this case. The authorities of the city and state deliberately inflamed the public mind to the point where they could not keep the peace without martial law. Responsible to nothing but their own corrupt conscience, the newspapers and the prosecution launched the ridiculous claim that the Communist Party was in some way linked to these two murders. Only here in court yesterday morning did the State's Attorney cease implying that Bigger Thomas was guilty of other crimes, crimes which he could not prove.

"The hunt for Bigger Thomas served as an excuse to terrorize the entire Negro population, to arrest hundreds of Communists, to raid labor union headquarters and workers' organizations. Indeed, the tone of the press, the silence of the church, the attitude of the prosecution and the stimulated temper of the people are of such a nature as to indicate that *more* than revenge is being sought upon a man who has committed a crime.

"What is the cause of all this high feeling and excitement? Is it the crime of Bigger Thomas? Were Negroes liked yesterday and hated today because of what he has done? Were labor unions and workers' halls raided solely because a Negro committed a crime? Did those white bones lying on that table evoke the grasp of horror that went up from the nation?

"Your Honor, you know that that is *not* the case! All of the factors in the present hysteria existed before Bigger Thomas was ever heard of. Negroes, workers, and labor unions were hated as much yesterday as they are today.

"Crimes of even greater brutality and horror have been committed in this city. Gangsters have killed and have gone free to kill again. But none of that brought forth an indignation to equal this.

"Your Honor, that mob did not come here of its own accord! It was *incited!* Until a week ago those people lived their lives as quietly as always.

"Who, then, fanned this latent hate into fury? Whose interest is that thoughtless and misguided mob serving?

"The State's Attorney knows, for he promised the Loop bankers that if he were re-elected demonstrations for relief would be stopped! The Governor of the state knows, for he has pledged the Manufacturers' Association that he would use troops against workers who went out on strike! The Mayor knows, for he told the merchants of the city that the budget would be cut down, that no new taxes would be imposed to satisfy the clamor of the masses of the needy!

"There is guilt in the rage that demands that this man's life be snuffed out quickly! There is fear in the hate and impatience which impels the action of the mob congregated upon the streets beyond that window! All of them—the mob and the mob-masters; the wire-pullers and the frightened; the leaders and their pet vassals—know and feel that their lives are built upon a historical deed of wrong against many people, people from whose lives they have bled their leisure and their luxury! Their feeling of guilt is as deep as that of the boy who sits here on trial today. Fear and hate and guilt are the keynotes of this drama!

"Your Honor, for the sake of this boy and myself, I wish I could bring to this Court evidence of a morally worthier nature. I wish I could say that love, ambition, jealousy, the quest for adventure, or any of the more romantic feelings were back of these two murders. If I could honestly invest the hapless actor in this fateful drama with feelings of a loftier cast, my task would be easier and I would feel confident of the outcome. The odds would be with me, for I would be appealing to men bound by common ideals to judge with pity and understanding one of their brothers who erred and fell in the struggle. But I have no choice in this matter. Life has cut this cloth; not I.

"We must deal here with the raw stuff of life, emotions and impulses and attitudes as yet unconditioned by the strivings of science and civilization. We must deal here with a first wrong which, when committed by us, was understandable and inevitable; and then we must deal with the long trailing black sense of guilt stemming from that wrong, a sense of guilt which self-interest and fear would not let us atone. And we must deal here with the hot blasts of hate engendered in others by that first wrong, and then the monstrous and horrible crimes flowing from that hate, a hate which has seeped down into the hearts and molded the deepest and most delicate sensibilities of multitudes.

"We must deal here with a dislocation of life involving millions of people, a dislocation so vast as to stagger the imagination; so fraught with tragic consequences as to make us rather not want to look at it or think of it; so old that we would rather try to view it as an order of nature and strive with uneasy conscience and false moral fervor to keep it so.

"We must deal here, on both sides of the fence, among whites as well as blacks, among workers as well as employers, with men and women in whose minds there loom good and bad of such height and weight that they assume proportions of abnormal aspect and construction. When situations like this arise, instead of men feeling that they are facing other men, they feel that they are facing mountains, floods, seas: forces of nature whose size and strength focus the minds and emotions to a degree of tension unusual in the quiet routine of urban life. Yet this tension exists within the limits of urban life, undermining it and supporting it in the same gesture of being.

"Allow me, Your Honor, before I proceed to cast blame and ask for mercy, to state emphatically that I do *not* claim that this boy is a victim of injustice, nor do I ask that this Court be sympathetic with him. That is not my object in embracing his character and his cause. It is not to tell you only of suffering that I stand here today, even though there are frequent lynchings and floggings of Negroes throughout the country. If you react only to that part of what I say, then you, too, are caught as much as he in the mire of blind emotion, and this vicious game will roll on, like a bloody river to a bloodier sea. Let us banish from our minds the thought that this is an unfortunate victim of injustice. The very concept of injustice rests upon a premise of equal claims, and this boy here today makes no claim upon you. If you think or feel that he does, then you, too, are blinded by a feeling as terrible as that which you condemn in him, and without as much justification. The feeling of guilt which has caused all of the mob-fear and mob-hysteria is the counterpart of his own hate.

"Rather, I plead with you to see a mode of *life* in our midst, a mode of life stunted and distorted, but possessing its own laws and claims, an existence of men growing out of the soil prepared by the collective but blind will of a hundred million people. I beg you to recognize human life draped in a form and guise alien to ours, but springing from a soil plowed and sown by all our hands. I ask you to recognize the laws and processes flowing from such a condition, understand them, seek to change them. If we do none of these, then we should not pretend horror or surprise when thwarted life expresses itself in fear and hate and crime.

"This is life, new and strange; strange, because we fear it; new, because we have kept our eyes turned from it. This is life lived in cramped limits and expressing itself not in terms of our good and bad, but in terms of its own fulfillment. Men are men and life is life, and we must deal with them as they are; and if we want to change them, we must deal with them in the form in which they exist and have their being.

"Your Honor, I must still speak in general terms, for the background of this boy must be shown, a background which has acted powerfully and importantly upon his conduct. Our forefathers came to these shores and faced a harsh and wild country. They came here with a stifled dream in their hearts, from lands where their personalities had been denied, as even we have denied the personality of this boy. They came from cities of the old world where the means to sustain life were hard to get or own. They were colonists and they were faced with a difficult choice: they had either to subdue this wild land or be subdued by it. We need but turn our eyes upon the imposing sweep of streets and factories and buildings to see how completely they have conquered. But in conquering they *used* others, used their lives. Like a miner using a pick or a carpenter using a saw, they bent the will of others to their own. Lives to them were tools and weapons to be wielded against a hostile land and climate.

"I do not say this in terms of moral condemnation. I do not say it to rouse pity in you for the black men who were slaves for two and one-half centuries. It would be foolish now to look back upon that in the light of injustice. Let us not be naïve: men do what they must, even when they feel that they are being driven by God, even when they feel they are fulfilling the will of God. Those men were engaged in a struggle for life and their choice in the matter was small indeed. It was the imperial dream of a feudal age that made men enslave others. Exalted by the will to rule, they could not have built nations on so vast a scale had they not shut their eyes to the humanity of other men, men whose lives were necessary for their building. But the invention and widespread use of machines made the further direct enslavement of men economically impossible, and so slavery ended.

"Let me, Your Honor, dwell a moment longer upon the danger of looking upon this boy in the light of injustice. If I should say that he is a victim of injustice, then I would be asking by implication for sympathy; and if one insists upon looking at this boy in the light of sympathy, he will be swamped by a feeling of guilt so strong as to be indistinguishable from hate.

"Of all things, men do not like to feel that they are guilty of wrong, and if you make them feel guilt, they will try desperately to justify it on any grounds; but, failing that, and seeing no immediate solution that will set things right without too much cost to their lives and property, they will kill that which evoked in them the condemning sense of guilt. And this is true of all men, whether they be white or black; it is a peculiar and powerful, but common, need.

"This guilt-fear is the basic tone of the prosecution and of the people in this case. In their hearts they feel that a wrong has been done and when a Negro commits a crime against them, they fancy they see the ghastly evidence of that wrong. So the men of wealth and property, the victims of attack who are eager to protect their profits, say to their guilty hirelings, 'Stamp out this ghost!' Or, like Mr. Dalton, they say, 'Let's do something for this man so he won't feel that way.' But then it is too late.

"If only ten or twenty Negroes had been put into slavery, we could call it injustice, but there were hundreds of thousands of them throughout the country. If this state of affairs had lasted for two or three years, we could say that it was unjust; but it lasted for more than two hundred years. Injustice which lasts for three long centuries and which exists among millions of people over thousands of square miles of territory, is injustice no longer; it is an accomplished fact of life. Men adjust themselves to their land; they create their own laws of being; their notions of right and wrong. A common way of earning a living gives them a common attitude toward life. Even their speech is colored and shaped by what they must undergo. Your Honor, injustice blots out one form of life, but another grows up in its place with its own rights, needs, and aspirations. What is happening here today is not injustice, but *oppression*, an attempt to throttle or stamp out a new form of life. And it is this new form of life that has grown up here in our midst that puzzles us, that expresses itself, like a weed growing from under a stone, in terms we call crime. Unless we grasp this problem in the light of this new reality, we cannot do more than salve our feelings of guilt and rage with more murder when a man, living under such conditions, commits an act which we call a crime.

"This boy represents but a tiny aspect of a problem whose reality sprawls over a third of this nation. Kill him! Burn the life out of him! And still when the delicate and unconscious machinery of race relations slips, there will be murder again. How can law contradict the lives of millions of people and hope to be administered successfully? Do we believe in magic? Do you believe that by burning a cross you can frighten a multitude, paralyze their will and impulses? Do you think that the white daughters in the homes of America will be any safer if you kill this boy? No! I tell you in all solemnity that they won't! The surest way to make certain that there will be more such murders is to kill this boy. In your rage and guilt, make thousands of other black men and women feel that the barriers are tighter and higher! Kill him and swell the tide of pent-up lava that will some day break loose, not in a single, blundering, accidental, individual crime, but in a wild cataract of emotion that will brook no control. The all-important thing for this Court to remember in deciding this boy's fate is that, though his crime was accidental, the emotions that broke loose were *already* there; the thing to remember is that this boy's way of life was a way of guilt; that his crime existed long before the murder of Mary Dalton; that the accidental nature of his crime took the guise of a sudden and violent rent in the veil behind which he lived, a rent which allowed his feelings of resentment and estrangement to leap forth and find objective and concrete form.

"Obsessed with guilt, we have sought to thrust a corpse from before our eyes. We have marked off a little plot of ground and buried it. We tell our souls in the deep of the black night that it is dead and that we have no reason for fear or uneasiness.

"But the corpse returns and raids our homes! We find our daughters murdered and burnt! And we say, 'Kill! Kill!'

"But, Your Honor, I say: 'Stop! Let us look at what we are doing!' For the corpse is not dead! It still lives! It has made itself a home in the wild forest of our great cities, amid the rank and choking vegetation of slums! It has forgotten our language! In order to live it has sharpened its claws! It has grown hard and calloused! It has developed a capacity for hate and fury which we cannot understand! Its movements are unpredictable! By night it creeps from its lair and steals toward the settlements of civilization! And at the sight of a kind face it does not lie down upon its back and kick up its heels playfully to be tickled and stroked. No; it leaps to kill!

"Yes, Mary Dalton, a well-intentioned white girl with a smile upon her face, came to Bigger Thomas to help him. Mr. Dalton, feeling vaguely that a social wrong existed, wanted to give him a job so that his family could eat and his sister and brother could go to school. Mrs. Dalton, trying to grope her way toward a sense of decency, wanted him to go to school and learn a trade. But when they stretched forth their helping hands, death struck! Today they mourn and wait for revenge. The wheel of blood continues to turn!

"I have only sympathy for those kind-hearted, white-haired parents. But to Mr. Dalton, who is a real estate operator, I say now: 'You rent houses to Negroes in the Black Belt and you refuse to rent to them elsewhere. You kept Bigger Thomas in that forest. You kept the man who murdered your daughter a stranger to her and you kept your daughter a stranger to him.'

"The relationship between the Thomas family and the Dalton family was that of renter to landlord, customer to merchant, employee to employer. The Thomas family got poor and the Dalton family got rich. And Mr. Dalton, a decent man, tried to salve his feelings by giving money. But, my friend, gold was not enough! Corpses cannot be bribed! Say to yourself, Mr. Dalton, 'I offered my daughter as a burnt sacrifice and it was not enough to push back into its grave this thing that haunts me.'

"And to Mrs. Dalton, I say: 'Your philanthropy was as tragically blind as your sightless eyes!'

"And to Mary Dalton, if she can hear me, I say: 'I stand here today trying to make your death *mean* something!'

"Let me, Your Honor, explain further the meaning of Bigger Thomas' life. In him and men like him is what was in our forefathers when they first came to these strange shores hundreds of years ago. We were lucky. They are not. We found a land whose tasks called forth the deepest and best we had; and we built a nation, mighty and feared. We poured and are still pouring our soul into it. But we have told them: 'This is a white man's country!' They are yet looking for a land whose tasks can call forth their deepest and best.

"Your Honor, consider the mere physical aspect of our civilization. How alluring, how dazzling it is! How it excites the senses! How it seems to dangle within easy reach of everyone the fulfillment of happiness! How constantly and overwhelmingly the advertisements, radios, newspapers and movies play upon us! But in thinking of them remember that to many they are tokens of mockery. These bright colors may fill our hearts with elation, but to many they are daily taunts. Imagine a man walking amid such a scene, a part of it, and yet knowing that it is *not* for him!

"We planned the murder of Mary Dalton, and today we come to court and say: 'We had nothing to do with it!' But every school teacher knows that this is not so, for every school teacher knows the restrictions which have been placed upon Negro education. The authorities know that it is not so, for they have made it plain in their every act that they mean to keep Bigger Thomas and his kind within rigid limits. All real estate operators know that it is not so, for they have agreed among themselves to keep Negroes within the ghetto-areas of cities. Your Honor, we who sit here today in this courtroom are witnesses. We know this evidence, for we helped to create it.

"But the question may be asked, 'If this boy thought that he was somehow wronged, why did he not go into a court of law and seek a redress of his grievances? Why should he take the law into his own hands?' Your Honor, this boy had no notion before he murdered, and he has none now, of having been wronged by any specific individuals. And, to be honest with you, the very life he has led created in him a frame of mind which makes him expect much less of this Court than you will ever know.

"This boy's crime was not an act of retaliation by an injured man against a person who he thought had injured him. If it were, then this case would be simple indeed. This is the case of a man's mistaking a whole race of men as a part of the natural structure of the universe and of his acting toward them accordingly. He murdered Mary Dalton accidentally, without thinking, without plan, without conscious motive. But, after he murdered, he accepted the crime. And that's the important thing. It was the first full act of his life; it was the most meaningful, exciting and stirring thing that had ever happened to him. He accepted it because it made him free, gave him the possibility of choice, of action, the opportunity to act and to feel that his actions carried weight.

"We are dealing here with an impulse stemming from deep down. We are dealing here not with how man acts toward man, but how a man acts when he feels that he must defend himself against, or adapt himself to, the total natural world in which he lives. The central fact to be understood here is not who wronged this boy, but what kind of a vision of the world did he have before his eyes, and where did he get such a vision as to make him, without premeditation, snatch the life of another person so quickly and instinctively that even though there was an element of accident in it, he was willing after the crime to say: 'Yes; I did it. I had to.'

"I know that it is the fashion these days for a defendant to say: 'Everything went blank to me.' But this boy does not say that. He says the opposite. He says he knew what he was doing but felt he *had* to do it. And he says he feels no sorrow for having done it.

"Do men regret when they kill in war? Does the personality of a soldier coming at you over the top of a trench matter?

"No! You kill to keep from being killed! And after a victorious war you return to a free country, just as this boy, with his hands stained with the blood of Mary Dalton, felt that he was free for the first time in his life.

"Multiply Bigger Thomas twelve million times, allowing for environmental and temperamental variations, and for those Negroes who are completely under the influence of the church, and you have the psychology of the Negro people. But once you see them as a whole, once your eyes leave the individual and encompass the mass, a new quality comes into the picture. Taken collectively, they are not simply twelve million people; in reality they constitute a separate nation, stunted, stripped, and held captive *within* this nation, devoid of political, social, economic, and property rights.

"Do you think that you can kill one of them—even if you killed one every day in the year—and make the others so full of fear that they would not kill? No! Such a foolish policy has never worked and never will. The more you kill the more you deny and separate, the more will they seek another form and way of life, however blindly and unconsciously. And out of what can they weave a different life, out of what can they mold a new existence, living organically in the same towns and cities, the same neighborhoods with us? I ask, out of what—but what we *are* and *own?*

"Your Honor, there are four times as many Negroes in America today as there were people in the original Thirteen Colonies when they struck for their freedom. These twelve million Negroes, conditioned broadly by our own notions as we were by European ones when we first came here, are struggling within unbelievably narrow limits to achieve that feeling of at-home-ness for which we once strove so ardently. And, compared with our own struggle, they are striving under conditions far more difficult. If anybody can, surely we ought to be able to understand what these people are after. This vast stream of life, damned and muddied, is trying to sweep toward the fulfillment which all of us seek so fondly, but find so impossible to put into words. When we said that men are 'endowed with certain inalienable rights, among those are life, liberty, and the pursuit of happiness,' we did not pause to define 'happiness.' That is the un-expressed quality in our quest, and we have never tried to put it into words. That is why we say, 'Let each man serve God in his own fashion.'

"But there are some broad features of the kind of happiness we are seeking which are known. We know that happiness comes to men when they are caught up, absorbed in a meaningful task or duty to be done, a task or duty which in turn sheds justification and sanction back down upon their humble labors. We know that this may take many forms: in religion it is the story of the creation of man, of his fall, and of his redemption; compelling men to order their lives in certain ways, all cast in terms of cosmic images and symbols which swallow the soul in fullness and wholeness. In art, science, industry, politics, and social action it may take other forms. But these twelve million Negroes have access to none of these highly crystallized modes of expression, save that of religion. And many of them know religion only in its most primitive form. The environment of tense urban centers has all but paralyzed the impulse for religion as a way of life for them today, just as it has for us.

"Feeling the capacity to be, to live, to act, to pour out the spirit of their souls into concrete and objective form with a high fervor born of their racial characteristics, they glide through our complex civilization like wailing ghosts; they spin like fiery planets lost from their orbits; they wither and die like trees ripped from native soil.

"Your Honor, remember that men can starve from a lack of self-realization as much as they can from a lack of bread! And they can *murder* for it, too! Did we not build a nation, did we not wage war and conquer in the name of a dream to realize our personalities and to make those realized personalities secure!

"But did Bigger Thomas really *murder?* At the risk of offending the sensibilities of this Court, I ask the question in the light of the ideals by which *we* live! Looked at from the outside, maybe it was murder; yes. But to him it was *not* murder. If it was murder, then what was the motive? The prosecution has shouted, stormed and threatened, but he has not said *why* Bigger Thomas killed! He has not said why because he does not know. The truth is, Your Honor, there was no motive as you and I understand motives within the scope of our laws today. The truth is, this boy did *not* kill! Oh, yes; Mary Dalton is dead. Bigger Thomas smothered her to death. Bessie Mears is dead. Bigger Thomas battered her with a brick in an abandoned building. But did he murder? Did he kill? Listen: what Bigger Thomas did early that Sunday morning in the Dalton home and what he did that Sunday night in that empty building was but a tiny aspect of what he had been doing all his life long! He was *living*, only as he knew how, and as we have forced him to live. The actions that resulted in the death of those two women were as instinctive and inevitable as breathing or blinking one's eyes. It was an act of *creation!*

"Let me tell you more. Before this trial the newspapers and the prosecution said that this boy had committed other crimes. It is true. He is guilty of numerous crimes. But search until the day of judgment, and you will find not one shred of evidence of them. He has murdered many times, but there are no corpses. Let me explain. This Negro boy's entire attitude toward life is a *crime!* The hate and fear which we have inspired in him, woven by our civilization into the very structure of his consciousness, into his blood and bones, into the hourly functioning of his personality, have become the justification of his existence.

"Every time he comes in contact with us, he kills! It is a physiological and psychological reaction, embedded in his being. Every thought he thinks is potential murder. Excluded from, and unassimilated in our society, yet longing to gratify impulses akin to our own but denied the objects and channels evolved through long centuries for their socialized expression, every sunrise and sunset make him guilty of subversive actions. Every movement of his body is an unconscious protest. Every desire, every dream, no matter how intimate or personal, is a plot or a conspiracy. Every hope is a plan for insurrection. Every glance of the eye is a threat. *His very existence is a crime against the state!*

"It so happened that that night a white girl was present in a bed and a Negro boy was standing over her, fascinated with fear, hating her; a blind woman walked into the room and that Negro boy killed that girl to keep from being discovered in a position which he knew *we* claimed warrants the death penalty. But that is only *one* side of it! He was impelled toward murder as much through the thirst for excitement, exultation, and elation as he was through fear! It was his way of *living!*

"Your Honor, in our blindness we have so contrived and ordered the lives of men that the moths in their hearts flutter toward ghoulish and incomprehensible flames!

"I have not explained the relationship of Bessie Mears to this boy. I have not forgotten her. I omitted to mention her until now because she was largely omitted from the consciousness of Bigger Thomas. His relationship to this poor black girl also reveals his relationship to the world. But Bigger Thomas is not here on trial for having murdered Bessie Mears. And he knows that. What does this mean? Does not the life of a Negro girl mean as much in the eyes of the law as the life of a white girl? Yes, perhaps, in the abstract. But under the stress of fear and flight, Bigger Thomas did not think of Bessie. He could not. The attitude of America toward this boy regulated his most intimate dealings with his own kind. After he had killed Mary Dalton, he killed Bessie Mears to silence her, to save himself. After he had killed Mary Dalton the fear of having killed a white woman filled him to the exclusion of everything else. He could not react to Bessie's death; his consciousness was determined by the fear that hung above him.

"But, one might ask, did he not love Bessie? Was she not his girl? Yes; she was his girl. He had to have a girl, so he had Bessie. But he did not love her. Is love possible to the life of a man I've described to this Court? Let us see. Love is not based upon sex alone, and that is all he had with Bessie. He wanted more, but the circumstances of his life and her life would not allow it. And the temperament of both Bigger and Bessie kept it out. Love grows from stable relationships, shared experience, loyalty, devotion, trust. Neither Bigger nor Bessie had any of these. What was there they could hope for? There was no common vision binding their hearts together; there was no common hope steering their feet in a common path. Even though they were intimately together, they were confoundingly alone. They were physically dependent upon each other and they hated that dependence. Their brief moments together were for purposes of sex. They loved each other as much as they hated each other; perhaps they hated each other more than they loved. Sex warms the deep roots of life; it is the soil out of which the tree of love grows. But these were trees without roots, trees that lived by the light of the sun and what chance rain that fell upon stony ground. Can disembodied spirits love? There existed between them fitful splurges of physical elation; that's all.

"Your Honor, is this boy alone in feeling deprived and baffled? Is he an exception? Or are there others? There are others. Your Honor, millions of others, Negro and white, and that is what makes our future seem a looming image of violence. The feeling of resentment and the balked longing for some kind of fulfilment and exultation—in degrees more or less intense and in actions more or less conscious—stalk day by day through this land. The consciousness of Bigger Thomas, and millions of others more or less like him, white and black, according to the weight of the pressure we have put upon them, forms the quicksands upon which the foundations of our civilization rest. Who knows when some slight shock, disturbing the delicate balance between social order and thirsty aspiration, shall send the skyscrapers in our cities toppling? Does that sound fantastic? I assure you that it is no more fantastic than those troops and that waiting mob whose presence and guilty anger portend something which we dare not even *think!*

"Your Honor, Bigger Thomas was willing to vote for and follow any man who would have led him out of his morass of pain and hate and fear. If that mob outdoors is afraid of *one* man, what will it feel if *millions* rise? How soon will someone speak the word that resentful millions will understand: the word to be, to act, to live? Is this Court so naïve as to think that they will not take a chance that is even less risky than that Bigger Thomas took? Let us not concern ourselves with that part of Bigger Thomas' confession that says he murdered accidentally, that he did not rape the girl. It really does not matter. What does matter is that he was guilty *before* he killed! That was why his whole life became so quickly and naturally organized, pointed, charged with a new meaning when this thing occurred. Who knows when another 'accident' involving millions of men will happen, an 'accident' that will be the dreadful day of our doom?

"Lodged in the heart of this moment is the question of power which time will unfold!

"Your Honor, another civil war in these states is not impossible; and if the misunderstanding of what this boy's life means is an indication of how men of wealth and property are misreading the consciousness of the submerged millions today, one may truly come.

"I do not propose that we try to solve this entire problem here in this court room today. That is not within the province of our duty, nor even, I think, within the scope of our ability. But our decision as to whether this black boy is to live or die can be made in accordance with what actually exists. It will at least indicate that we *see* and *know!* And our seeing and knowing will comprise a consciousness of how inescapably this one man's life will confront us ten million fold in the days to come.

"I ask that you spare this boy, send him to prison for life. What would prison mean to Bigger Thomas? It holds advantages for him that a life of freedom never had. To send him to prison would be more than an act of mercy. You would be for the first time conferring *life* upon him. He would be brought for the first time within the orbit of our civilization. He would have an identity, even though it be but a number. He would have for the first time an openly designated relationship with the world. The very building in which he would spend the rest of his natural life would be the best he has ever known. Sending him to prison would be the first recognition of his personality he has ever had. The long black empty years ahead would constitute for his mind and feelings the only certain and durable object around which he could build a meaning for his life. The other inmates would be the first men with whom he could associate on a basis of equality. Steel bars between him and the society he offended would provide a refuge from hate and fear.

"I say, Your Honor, give this boy his life. And in making this concession we uphold those two fundamental concepts of our civilization, those two basic concepts upon which we have built the mightiest nation in history—personality and security—the conviction that the person is inviolate and that which sustains him is equally so.

"Let us not forget that the magnitude of our modern life, our railroads, power plants, ocean liners, airplanes, and steel mills flowered from these two concepts, grew from our dream of creating an invulnerable base upon which man and his soul can stand secure.

"Your Honor, this Court and those troops are not the real agencies that keep the public peace. Their mere presence is proof that we are letting peace slip through our fingers. Public peace is the act of public trust; it is the faith that *all* are secure and will *remain* secure.

"When men of wealth urge the use and show of force, quick death, swift revenge, then it is to protect a little spot of private security against the resentful millions from whom they have filched it, the resentful millions in whose militant hearts the dream and hope of security still lives.

"Your Honor, I ask in the name of all we are and believe, that you spare this boy's life! With every atom of my being, I beg this in order that not only may this black boy live, but that we ourselves may not die!"

Carrie A. Young

was born in Lynchburg, Virginia, but
it was in Montclair, New Jersey that
she first saw a burning cross, symbol
of the KKK. She went to college in
the South and in the North and is
now doing social work in a foster
care agency in New York City. *Adjö
Means Goodbye* is her first published
story.

Adjö means goodbye

IT HAS been a long time since I knew Marget Swenson. How the years have rushed by! I was a child when I knew her, and now I myself have children. The circle keeps turning, keeps coming full.

The mind loses many things as it matures, but I never lost Marget; she has remained with me, like the first love and the first hurt. The mind does not lose what is meaningful to one's existence. Marget was both my first love and first hurt. I met her when she joined our sixth-grade class.

She stood before the class holding tightly to the teacher's hand, her blue, frightened eyes sweeping back and forth across the room until they came to rest on my face. From that very first day we became friends. Marget, just fresh from Sweden, and me, a sixth generation American. We were both rather shy and quiet and perhaps even lonely, and that's why we took to each other. She spoke very little English, but somehow we managed to understand each other. We visited one another at home practically every day. My young life had suddenly become deliciously complete. I had a dear friend.

Sometimes we talked and laughed on the top of the big, dazzling green hill close to the school. We had so much to talk about; so many things were new to her. She asked a thousand questions and I—I, filled to bursting with pride that it was from me that she wished to learn, responded eagerly and with excesses of superlatives.

Now, sometimes, when I drive my children to school and watch them race up the walks to the doors, I wonder what lies ahead in the momentary darkness of the hall corridors, and think of Marget once more. I think of how she came out of a dark corridor one day, the day she really looked at my brother when she was visiting me. I saw her following him with new eyes, puzzled eyes, and a strange fear gripped me. "Your brother," she whispered to me, "is African?"

I was a little surprised and a little hurt. Didn't we cheer for Tarzan when we went to the movies? Were not the Africans always frightened and cowardly? But I answered, "No silly," and I continued to wait.

"He looks different from you."

"He should," I said, managing to laugh. My brother *was* darker than anyone else in the family. "He's a boy and I'm a girl. But we're both Negro, of course."

She opened her mouth to say something else, then closed it and the fear slipped away.

Marget lived up on the hill. That was the place where there were many large and pretty houses. I suppose it was only in passing that I knew only white people lived there. Whenever I visited, Marget's mother put up a table in their garden, and Marget and I had milk and *kaka,* a kind of cake. Mrs. Swenson loved to see me eat. She was a large, round woman, with deep blue eyes and very red cheeks. Marget, though much smaller, of course, looked quite like her. We did our homework after we had the cake and milk, compositions or story reading. When we finished, Mrs. Swenson hugged me close and I knew I was loved in that home. A child knows when it is loved or only tolerated. But I was loved. Mrs. Swenson thanked me with a thick, Swedish accent for helping Marget.

Marget and I had so much fun with words, and there were times when we sat for hours in my garden or hers, or on the hilltop, surrounded by grass and perhaps the smell of the suppers being prepared for our fathers still at work downtown. Her words were Swedish, mine, English. We were surprised how much alike many of them sounded, and we laughed at the way each of us slid our tongues over the unfamiliar words. I learned the Swedish equivalents of mother, father, house, hello, friend, and goodbye.

One day Marget and I raced out of school as soon as the ringing bell released us. We sped down the hill, flashed over gray concrete walks and green lawns dotted with dandelions and scattered daises, our patent leather buckled shoes slapping a merry tattoo as we went, our long stockings tumbling down our legs. We were going to Marget's to plan her birthday party. Such important business for 10-year-olds!

Eventually, after much planning and waiting, the day of the party came. I put on my pink organdy dress with the Big Bertha collar, and a new pair of patent leather shoes that tortured my feet unbearably. Skipping up the hill to Marget's, I stopped at a lawn which looked deserted. I set down my gift and began to pick the wild flowers that were growing there. Suddenly, from out of nowhere, an old man appeared. "What do you think you're doing, pulling up my flowers?" he shouted. Once again I held myself tightly against the fear, awaiting that awful thing that I felt must come. "I wanted to take them to my friend," I explained. "She's having a birthday today."

The old man's eyes began to twinkle. "She is, is she? Well, you just wait a minute, young lady." He went away and came back with garden shears and cut a handfull and then an armfull of flowers, and with a smile sent me on my way. My childish fears had been ambushed by a kindness.

I arrived at the party early and Marget and I whizzed around, putting the finishing touches on the decorations. There were hardly enough vases for all the flowers the old man had given me. Some fifteen minutes later the doorbell rang and Marget ran around to the front, saying, "Oh, here they come!"

But it was Mary Ann, another girl in our class, and she was alone. She put her present for Marget on the table and the three of us talked. Occasionally, Marget got up and went around to the front to see who had come unheralded by the doorbell. No one.

"I wonder what's taking them so long?" Mary Ann asked.

Growing more upset by the minute, Marget answered, "Maybe they didn't remember what time the party was."

How does a child of ten describe a sense of foreboding, the feeling that the bad things have happened because of herself? I sat silently, waiting.

When it got to be after five, Mrs. Swenson called Marget inside; she was there for a long time, and when she came out, she looked very, very sad. "My mother does not think they are coming," she said.

"Why not?" Mary Ann blurted.

"Betty Hatcher's mother was here last night and she talked a long time with my mother. I thought it was about the party. Mother kept saying, 'Yes, yes, she is coming'."

I took Marget's hand. "Maybe they were talking about me," I said. Oh! I remember so painfully today how I wanted her quick and positive denial to that thrust of mine into darkness where I knew something alive was lurking. Although she did it quite casually, I was aware that Marget was trying to slip her hand from mine, as though she might have had the same thought I had voiced aloud. I opened my hand and let her go. "Don't be silly," she said.

No one came. The three of us sat in the middle of rows and rows of flowers and ate our ice cream and cake. Our pretty dresses, ribbons and shoes were dejected blobs of color. It was as if the world had swung out around us and gone past, leaving us whole, but in some way indelibly stamped forever.

It was different between Marget and me after her birthday. She stopped coming to my house, and when at school I asked her when she would, she looked as though she would cry. She had to do something for her mother, was her unvarying excuse. So, one day, I went to her house, climbed up the hill where the old man had picked the flowers, and a brooding, restless thing grew within me at every step, almost a *knowing*. I had not, after all, been invited to Marget's. My throat grew dry and I thought about turning back, and for the first time the hill and all the homes looked alien, even threatening to me.

Marget almost jumped when she opened the door. She stared at me in shock. Then, quickly, in a voice I'd never heard before, she said, "My mother says you can't come to my house anymore."

I opened my mouth, and closed it without speaking. The awful thing had come; the knowing was confirmed. Marget, crying, closed the door in my face. When I turned to go down the stairs and back down the hill to my house, my eyes, too, were filled with tears. No one had to tell me that the awful thing had come because Marget was white and I was not. I just *knew it* deep within myself. I guess I expected it to happen. It was only a question of when.

June. School was coming to a close. Those days brimmed with strange, uncomfortable moments when Marget and I looked at each other and our eyes darted quickly away. We were little pawns, one white, one colored, in a game over which we had no control then. We did not speak to each other at all.

On the last day of school, I screwed up a strange and reckless courage and took my autograph book to where Marget was sitting. I handed it to her. She hesitated, then took it, and without looking up, wrote words I don't remember now; they were quite common words, the kind every one was writing in every one else's book. I waited. Slowly, she passed her book to me and in it I wrote with a slow, firm hand some of the words she had taught me. I wrote *Adjö min vän.* Goodbye, my friend. I released her, let her go, told her not to worry; told her that I no longer needed her. *Adjö.*

Whenever I think of Marget now, and I do at the most surprising times, I wonder if she ever thinks of me, if she is married and has children, and I wonder if she has become a queen by now, instead of a pawn.

A Postscript
concerning the times

BEYOND THE ANGRY BLACK was in preparation during America's longest, hottest, summer, so far. It is strange how quickly and widely that phrase gained credence all over the world. The originator of it, the late William Faulkner, must have some restless moments, wherever he is, whenever it is used to describe the warm-weather campaigns of the Negro Revolution—still another phrase ground off the assembly line by white Americans.

The only Negro-originated phrase I've heard during my year away from the United States, is black power; most of the press capitalizes the 'b' in 'black' and the 'p' in 'power.' The term is the creation of the late Richard Wright who, like Faulkner, was a Mississippian. Call it fate. Wright's *Native Son* is included in part in this volume as *The Plea*. Black power was at once shaded and then loaded with meaning by the press for the purpose of, apparently, creating still more (and perhaps even necessary) tension to the American racial situation which is rapidly becoming an insoluble problem.

Much has happened in America since the first edition of his collection appeared in 1962; one cannot say this too often, and one can never say it without amazement. The period from autumn, 1965 to autumn 1966 proved only that not nearly enough has happened, however, for Afro-Americans, and that too much has happened for the mixed bag of other, white, hyphenated Americans. That period has also proved it likely that Mr. Faulkner's phrase may soon be applicable not only to summer, but to autumn, winter and spring as well. Unfortunately.

It seems to me that reason has run out.

It appears that Negroes and whites alike, whites having hardly allowed reason to enter the picture at all, and Negroes finding that their use of it is mistaken repeatedly for weakness, are about to discard it altogether. The reason that I thought lay beyond anger has been given extremely short shrift, with the result that we are already, without noticing it, in another, highly volatile area.

One must dread the next stretch of the future, for it is obvious that laws passed to bring equality closer to reality seem to come with the explosions of violence. Yet, that same violence, in every case touched off by whites—a policeman employing poor judgment, the murder of children in Sunday school, peaceful demonstrations—appears to be angering state and federal lawmakers. Obviously, whatever they did in the near past, they thought quite sufficient. They never intended to go the whole hog. Those laws benefited some Negroes, of course, but they in no way affected changes in the lives of the mass. Now, disenchantment, even lack of understanding, has set in among many whites who eagerly marched to Washington in 1963, or even marched from Selma to Montgomery in 1965.

That black Americans have contributed immensely to the nation for the almost five hundred years that they've been here from Africa is old hat. Cliche, like dying in Vietnam. I'm not going to repeat the list of those achievements here; they have been listed before, many, many times over, and now are only important to those Americans who happen to be black instead of white. What is important and needs setting down is the obvious conclusion that Negroes are not going to give damn much more without some return payment from someone or from something.

Let us face a hard fact here, now, in this year, 1966: what is wrong lies almost beyond the grasp of the mind; what is wrong rises out of the unknown dark epochs during which occurred the mutation that created which race—black or white?

The fear that lashes the white populations of the entire earth— and it is a groundless, irrational fear, proved so ten thousand times over—had to have had its origins in a time the mind can no longer perceive. This fear, which continues to reject all scientific assurances that it is groundless, has exterminated reason and brought us to a clearing. Is this where peace, finally, is to be made, or is it the place for the awful opposite

?

Amsterdam, Sept. 8, 1966

John A. Williams *published his first book six years ago (1960). Since then, he has produced eight books, three of them novels. One of his non-fiction works was published in 1964 under a pen name. His fourth novel and ninth book is to be published in Spring, 1967.*

His short fiction began to appear in 1957 in Dude *and* Gent; *subsequent publications in this genre have been seen in* Negro Digest, Province Town Review, *and many other little magazines, as well as in anthologies.*

Mr. Williams was a regular contributor to the New York Herald Tribune's *Book Week, and has either reviewed for or contributed articles to more than fifteen other newspapers. In addition, other articles have appeared in many magazines including* Holiday, Saturday Review, The New Leader *and* Ebony.

A former Director of Information for The American Committee on Africa, *Mr. Williams travelled widely in Africa for* Newsweek *in 1964, and returned in 1965 to film a television show in which he appeared and for which he wrote the script.*

He has lived abroad for short periods, the latest for a year, during which, in Spain, he co-produced a television show with Henry Roth, author of Call It Sleep. *All in all, he has visited 25 countries on three continents.*

In 1962, Mr. Williams was awarded a Grant from the National Institute of Arts and Letters for his second novel, Night Song. *He accepted the Grant a number of months after it had been awarded, because of a controversy surrounding his prior selection as the winner of the Prix de Rome, which was refused him. Mr. Williams' acceptance came only when the American Academy of Arts and Letters, affiliated with Rome and the NIAL, cancelled the Prix de Rome Creative Writing Fellowship.* Night Song, *which has since been published in seven editions in the United States and abroad, has been adapted for the film. Mr. Williams was also a Bread Loaf Scholar in 1960.*

Born near Jackson, Mississippi in 1925 and raised in Syracuse, New York, where he went to the University, Mr. Williams is married and has two sons from a previous marriage. He is a sports fan, an outdoorsman and an amateur geologist.